Scrap Quilts Go Country

Deanne Eisenman

Martingale®
& COMPANY

Scrap Quilts Go Country
© 2011 by Deanne Eisenman

That Patchwork Place® is an imprint
of Martingale & Company®.

Martingale & Company
19021 120th Ave. NE, Suite 102
Bothell, WA 98011-9511 USA
www.martingale-pub.com

Printed in China
16 15 14 13 12 11   8 7 6 5 4 3 2 1

Library of Congress
Cataloging-in-Publication Data
is available upon request.

ISBN: 978-1-60468-016-4

Mission Statement
*Dedicated to providing quality products
and service to inspire creativity.*

Credits
President & CEO ✦ Tom Wierzbicki
Editor in Chief ✦ Mary V. Green
Managing Editor ✦ Tina Cook
Developmental Editor ✦ Karen Costello Soltys
Technical Editor ✦ Nancy Mahoney
Copy Editor ✦ Liz McGehee
Design Director ✦ Stan Green
Production Manager ✦ Regina Girard
Illustrator ✦ Laurel Strand
Cover & Text Designer ✦ Regina Girard
Photographer ✦ Brent Kane
Special thanks to Vicki and Matt Howe of
Redmond, Washington for generously
allowing us to photograph in their home.

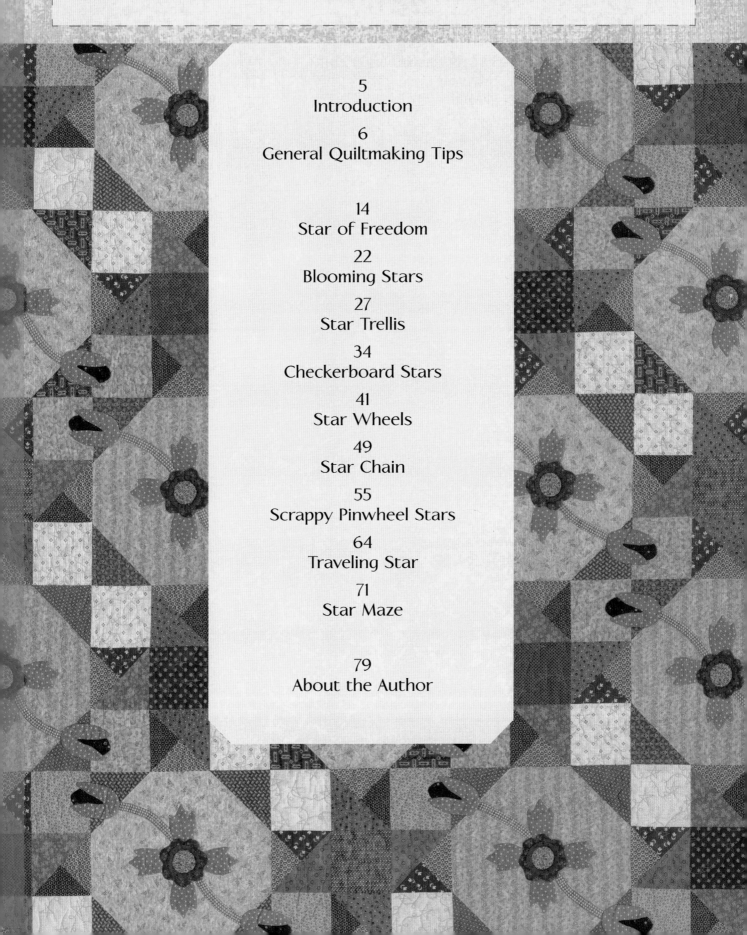

Contents

Introduction

I often think of the word "serendipity" when making scrap quilts. I feel the definition, the ability to make fortunate discoveries by accident, describes scrap quilts quite nicely. While choosing fabrics for scrap quilts, I have pulled different-colored fabric pieces from my stash and thought that there was no way those could coexist in the same project. But, as I laid them out on my cutting table, I began to see that they looked good together. A happy accident! I know we've all done this at one time or another.

For many years I've collected colorful fat quarters and fat eighths. On occasion, I've also purchased yardage without a specific project in mind. That was mostly because the fabric "caught my eye" or "I just had to have it!" I'm sure that sounds familiar to a lot of quilters. Often, I cut that yardage into fat quarters or 2½" strips to use at a later time. This habit allowed me to acquire quite a large stash, so I decided to design several scrappy patterns using mostly fat quarters or strips. If you enjoy a simple pieced project or one that includes piecing and appliqué, then this book is for you!

General Quiltmaking Tips

In more than 20 years of quilting, I've learned many tips and techniques that I'll share with you in this section. There is always the opportunity to learn from your small quilting group or your quilt guild. Take classes whenever you get the opportunity, even if you think you're a more-experienced quilter. You may be surprised and learn some other way to do something. I'm still learning new things all the time, sometimes wishing I had learned them a little sooner!

Color Basics

While I'm no expert on color theory, I can share a few basic terms and their meanings to help in picking out colors for your project. Having knowledge of color basics helps a great deal in planning scrap quilts.

+ **Hue:** the actual color of the fabric. Blue, red, and green are examples of hues.
+ **Analogous colors:** colors that are next to each other on the color wheel. Putting these colors together creates the least amount of contrast.
+ **Complementary colors:** colors that are directly opposite each other on the color wheel. Putting these colors together creates the greatest amount of contrast.
+ **Value:** relative lightness or darkness of a color. When we say a color is light, medium, or dark, we are talking about value or brightness.
+ **Tint:** when white is added to a hue to get a lighter version of the hue.
+ **Shade:** when black is added to a hue to get a darker version of the hue.

When picking fabrics for a scrappy quilt, it's best to first decide on a core group of colors (hues) you want to use, and then expand from there into different values, tints, and shades to create the scrappy look you desire. A scrappy quilt can be made subtle by using tints and shades of analogous colors close in value, or it can be made bold by using tints and shades of complementary colors in opposing values. If you wish to study color theory more in depth, there are many great books on color as it relates to quiltmaking.

HANDY COLOR TIP

For a lot of my projects, I have you cut a specific piece for a block from several different fabrics. Careful planning will help you determine how many pieces to cut from each fabric to get the desired distribution. For example, if you had a quilt with 12 blocks and each block had eight 2½" squares that needed to be cut from four different fabrics, the cutting instructions would be: From the 4 dark fat quarters, cut 96 squares, 2½" x 2½".

To determine how many squares to cut from each dark fat quarter, the math would be: 96 divided by 4 equals 24 squares from each fat quarter. If you used six dark fat quarters instead of four in the above example, you would divide 96 by 6 and cut 16 squares from each fat quarter. See how that works? It will take a little thinking and math to determine how many pieces to cut from the different fabrics. I promise it's easy math—no calculus here!

The best thing to do is plan how you want your blocks to look before cutting. I do this by drawing the quilt top on paper and using colored pencils to decide color placement. Most of the quilts in this book are made from one repeating block or two alternating blocks. When I plan color in a quilt, I draw one block and color in the different pieces to get the effect I like.

For example, in a quilt with 12 blocks, I may want to make 6 blocks using one color family, another 6 blocks in a different color family, and then alternate them when piecing the top. Or, I may want all 12 blocks to be the same with three or four different colors in each block. This is where sketch pads, design walls, and even computer programs come in handy! Depending on how you distribute the color, a scrap quilt can look slightly scrappy to very scrappy. It's all a matter of choice.

Prewashing Fabric

Prewashing your fabric *before* cutting it into strips or cutting specific pieces is a matter of personal preference. I generally prewash my fabrics if they're being used in a project that will be laundered often or if I'm worried about shrinkage or excess dyes in the fabric. I wash my fabric on the gentle cycle, taking care to separate darks and lights, and tumble dry on low. I remove the fabric from the dryer when it's still slightly damp, and then press it to remove wrinkles. To minimize fraying, consider trimming the raw edges with pinking shears before washing. If you like the "antique" look that fabric shrinkage creates, then you may not want to prewash. If you don't prewash the fabric, use a dye-catcher sheet, available from your grocery store, when laundering the quilt.

Rotary Cutting

Except for appliqué template pieces and where noted, all cutting instructions for the projects in this book are for rotary cutting. All measurements include ¼"-wide seam allowances. For detailed rotary-cutting information, look for books available at your local quilt shop or library.

CUTTING TIPS

✦ Before starting a project, make sure your rotary blade is sharp. A dull blade will cause skips in the cutting and make it harder to cut in general. If you find you have to press down hard to get a decent cut, your blade is probably ready for replacement.

✦ Remember the old adage "measure twice, cut once." The projects in this book allow some additional fabric for shrinkage and errors, but other books and patterns may not. If you're unsure of your cutting skills or whether the pattern you're using allows for extra fabric, you may want to add an additional ⅛ yard to the required amount for "wiggle room." It's a good idea to cut and then label all your pieces with the dimensions prior to sewing. I like to do this so that I'm sure I have enough fabric up front. No surprises!

✦ I like to cut the widest strips and width-of-fabric strips first. This way, if there is fabric left from a wider or longer strip, a smaller piece can be cut from it. I find there is less fabric waste this way.

Machine Piecing

Along with cutting accurately sized pieces, using proper techniques for machine piecing and pressing will help you achieve a successful finished project. In this section you'll find my thoughts on these subjects as well as instructions for techniques used throughout the book. Unless otherwise stated in a pattern, use a ¼" seam allowance when sewing two pieces together. For more information on machine-piecing techniques, look for books available at your local quilt shop or library.

HANDY MACHINE-PIECING TIPS

✦ Make sure your sewing-machine needle is in good shape before beginning a project. It's usually a good idea to change your needle after each project. The wear and tear on the needle may not be noticeable to you, but it's there.

✦ I usually use a light-colored neutral thread to piece my tops, unless I'm making a very dark quilt. In that case, I use a dark color that blends in, such as brown or black.

TRIANGLE SQUARES

Triangle squares (also called half-square-triangle units) are squares that are half one color and half another color. They can be created two at a time from two different colored squares. The squares are cut ⅞" larger than the finished size of the triangle square. For example, if your finished triangle square measures 2", the squares are cut 2⅞".

1. Cut two squares, one of each fabric, to the size specified in the cutting list. Draw a diagonal line from corner to corner on the wrong side of the lighter square.

2. Layer the two squares right sides together with the marked square on top and raw edges aligned.

3. Sew a scant ¼" on each side of the drawn line, making sure the squares are directly on top of each other and don't shift while sewing. Cut the squares apart on the drawn line. Press the seam allowances toward the darker fabric. Each pair of squares will yield two triangle squares.

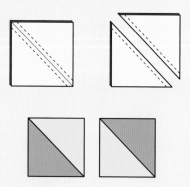

FOLDED-CORNER TECHNIQUE

For some of the projects in this book, I use the folded-corner technique to add an angled piece to the corner(s) of squares or rectangles. With folded corners, you can create complicated-looking units using just squares and rectangles. Smaller squares are marked and sewn to the corners of larger squares or rectangles.

1. Fold the smaller square in half diagonally, wrong sides together, or draw a diagonal line from corner to corner on the wrong side of the square.

2. With right sides together, lay the marked square in the corner of the larger square or rectangle with the line positioned as shown. Line up the raw edges. Sew on the marked line. Trim ¼" from the stitched line. Press the resulting triangle toward the corner and press the seam allowances open. Repeat on as many corners of the square or rectangle as instructed for the project.

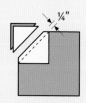

This folded-corner technique is also used to make flying-geese units that are used in many of the projects.

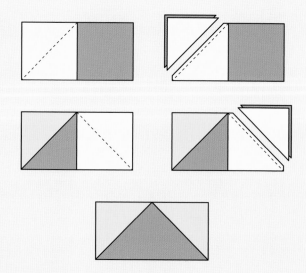

STRIP SETS

Some projects in this book will have you assemble a strip set. A strip set has two or more fabric strips that are joined along their long edges, and then smaller pieces are cut from the joined set. This is a quick way to make pieces for four-patch, nine-patch, or rail-fence units instead of having to piece together each individual square or rectangle.

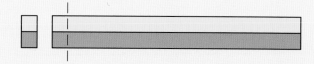

Pressing

The general rule in quilting is to press the seam allowances to one side, usually toward the darker fabric if possible. This makes the seams stronger than if the seam allowances were pressed open. Sometimes, a seam allowance may have to be pressed open to reduce bulk in an area of a block or quilt. This is usually the case where several seams meet. I'm a little unorthodox in this area since I've always pressed my seam allowances open. This was how I was taught many years ago, and I've been unable to break the habit!

Appliqué

There are many techniques for appliqué, and it would take many pages to describe them all, so I've chosen to give you one hand-appliqué method and one machine-appliqué method as well as instructions for making bias stems. Use one of these techniques or your own preferred method with any pattern that has appliqué. Appliqué templates do not include seam allowances.

NEEDLE-TURN HAND APPLIQUÉ

I took a few classes in hand appliqué before ever doing any type of machine appliqué, so I like doing hand appliqué the best. Oddly enough, it's the way I relax! That probably seems funny to those of you who are afraid of the "A word," as appliqué is sometimes called. You'll need appliqué needles, template material (I use paper or cardstock if the template will be used several times), scissors for cutting out the template, chalk pencils, small sewing scissors, thread that matches the color of the appliqué piece, water-soluble fabric glue, and very good lighting.

1. Trace the pattern onto the template material and cut it out.

2. Lay the template on the right side of the appropriate fabric and trace around it with a chalk pencil.

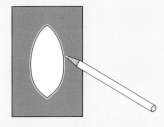

3. Cut out the shape from the fabric, adding a scant ¼" seam allowance.

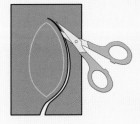

4. Clip the seam allowance, stopping one or two threads from the drawn line. Clips should be about 1" apart in straight areas and about ⅛" apart in curved areas. Clipping helps the appliqué maintain its shape when you turn under the seam allowance while sewing.

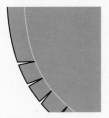

5. Dot the wrong side of the appliqué piece with just enough fabric glue to hold the appliqué piece in place so that it doesn't shift while stitching. Do not apply any glue in the seam allowance. Position the appliqué piece on the background fabric where indicated.

6. Turn under a small portion of the seam allowance. Thread your needle and knot one end. Bring the needle up from the wrong side of the fabric, catching a few threads on the edge of the appliqué. Then, insert the needle into the background fabric right next to where it came up but slightly underneath the appliqué. This creates a tiny blind stitch. Continue in this manner, turning under a small portion of seam allowance at a time and taking stitches about ⅛" (or less) apart. Anything wider between stitches can create puckers in the appliqué piece. Make a small knot on the back of the piece when you have stitched down the entire piece.

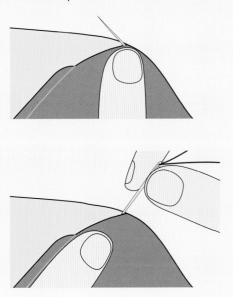

FUSIBLE-WEB MACHINE APPLIQUÉ

I admit that I'm not an expert in machine appliqué and use it very rarely, even though it generally is an easier and quicker method. The main difference from hand appliqué is that the appliqué piece is cut out without adding a seam allowance. The piece is positioned on the background, adhered with fusible web, and then stitched around the edges. You will need lightweight, paper-backed fusible web and thread. Use clear thread if you want the stitches to be invisible; use contrasting thread if you prefer that the stitches show. Because this process will produce shapes that are the reverse of the pattern, you'll need to make a mirror image of any shapes that aren't symmetrical. You can do this by tracing the pattern onto a piece of copy paper and then turning the paper over and tracing the pattern through to the blank side.

1. Trace the reversed patterns onto the paper side of the fusible web as many times as needed for each pattern. Leave about ½" of space between the motifs.

2. Cut out each shape roughly ¼" outside the drawn lines. If you'll be cutting more than one motif from the same fabric, cut out the group as a unit.

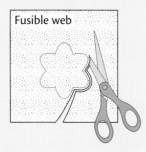

Fusible web

3. Place the fusible-web shapes on the wrong side of the appropriate fabrics. Follow the manufacturer's instructions to fuse the shapes in place. Cut out each shape on the traced line.

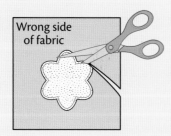

Wrong side of fabric

4. Remove the paper backing from the appliqué shapes. Position each shape on the background fabric where indicated, web side down, and press it in place with your iron.

5. Use a narrow zigzag stitch, blanket stitch, or other decorative stitch to stitch around the outside edges of each appliqué to permanently secure it.

MAKING BIAS STEMS

Strips cut on the bias stretch easily, making them ideal to use for appliqué stems that need to curve. The patterns in this book use bias strips cut from fat eighths or fat quarters. The strips are cut 1" wide and finish to ½".

1. Iron your piece of fabric to remove any wrinkles or folds.

2. Lay the fabric on the cutting surface with the longest edge closest to you. Place the 45°-angle mark of the ruler along the fabric's bottom edge. If your ruler isn't long enough to go the entire length of the fabric piece, butt another ruler against the end of the first so you have a continuous cutting guide. Once you have the ruler(s) aligned, hold it in place with your hand and make the diagonal cut with the rotary cutter.

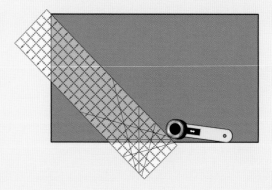

3. Align the 1" line on your ruler with the cut edge. Cut a strip. Cut as many strips as necessary to reach the total required length.

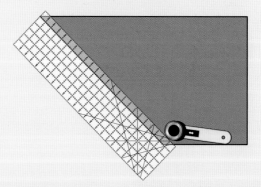

4. Once the strips are cut, you can trim them to the length needed or piece them together at right angles to achieve the required length.

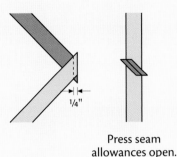

1/4"

Press seam allowances open.

5. To make stems from bias strips, press under ¼" on both long sides of the strip so that the raw edges meet in the center on the wrong side of the strip. A bias-tape maker or pressing bar makes this task easier.

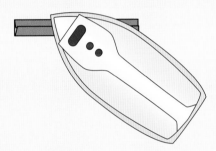

6. Place the stem on the background fabric, raw edges down. Machine or hand appliqué the stem in place along the long edges, beginning with the side that curves inward.

Border Strips

For many of the projects, I recommend you wait to cut the border strips to the required length until after the quilt top is pieced. Because each quilter's seam allowance may vary slightly, your quilt top may be a different size from what's indicated in the pattern. If that happens, by waiting to trim the border to the correct length, you'll be spared the headache of having to recut strips and possibly run out of fabric. Follow these instructions when cutting and adding borders to your quilt:

1. Lay the quilt top out on a large, flat surface— generally, a floor works best—and smooth out any wrinkles. Measure the length of the quilt top from top to bottom through the center to determine the length of the side border strips.

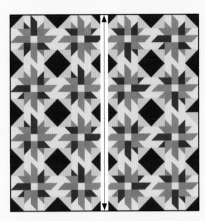

Measure vertically through center.

2. Cut border strips the width indicated in the project instructions. I generally cut border strips crosswise, selvage to selvage, and join two strips along their short ends with a straight seam to achieve the desired length. Using the measurement from step 1, calculate the length of each strip as follows: If the center measurement is 63", for example, 63 divided by 2 equals 31½. When joining two strips together, you need to add a ¼" seam allowance to each strip. Therefore, to make two 63"-long border strips, you need four strips 31¾" long.

3. Join the border strips to the sides of the quilt top and then, once again, lay the quilt top on a flat surface. Measure the width of the quilt top from side to side through the center (including the side borders). Repeat the process, trimming four border strips to the correct length and joining them in pairs to make two border strips, one for the top and one for the bottom of the quilt. Sew the strips in place.

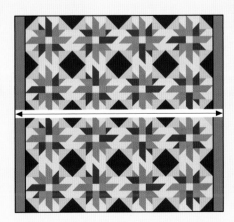

Measure horizontally through center.

Finishing Techniques

This is great! You've finished your quilt top. Now there are just a few more steps to make your quilt top into a completed quilt to enjoy.

LAYERING THE QUILT

To prepare the quilt for quilting, you need to layer the quilt top with batting and backing to make a quilt sandwich. The backing and batting pieces need to be at least 4" larger than your quilt top on each side. For larger quilts, you may need to piece two or three lengths together to make a backing that is large enough. The yardage given in the materials list for each project is based on 42"-wide fabric, but if you prefer not to piece your backing, wide-width backing fabrics are available. Just be sure to recalculate the yardage needed. If you're using a long-arm quilting service, be sure to check with the quilter because she may have her own specific preparation requirements.

1. Lay your backing fabric on a clean, flat surface, wrong side up. Smooth out any wrinkles. Use masking tape around the edges to secure it in place.

2. Lay the batting over the backing and smooth out any wrinkles.

3. Center the pressed quilt top over the batting. Smooth out any wrinkles and make sure the quilt-top edges are parallel to the edges of the backing. Baste the layers together by using either a large basting stitch or rustproof safety pins.

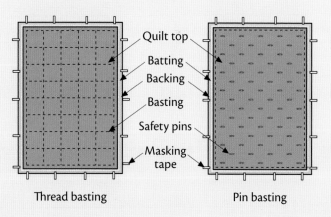

Quilt top
Batting
Backing
Basting
Safety pins
Masking tape

Thread basting   Pin basting

QUILTING

Many patterns will end the instructions with "quilt as desired." What exactly does that mean? If you haven't quilted much, it's not easy to figure out what quilting design to use on the quilt top. In this book, I describe how I've quilted the samples to provide some guidance. All of my projects are machine quilted, either on a home sewing machine or on a long-arm quilting machine. Here are some of the quilting techniques you can do by machine:

✦ **Stitch in the ditch.** Quilt along the seam lines.

✦ **Echo quilting.** Outline patchwork or appliqué designs to make them stand out.

✦ **Template quilting.** Mark a design on the quilt top using a template, and then quilt on the marked lines.

✦ **Meandering or free-motion quilting.** I use this method the most and generally quilt allover designs of curlicues and stars.

These methods can also be used when hand quilting. I don't hand quilt very well; I'm what you call a "stab stitcher," and I'm very slow. Therefore, I won't offer any advice on hand quilting, except to say there are some very good books on the subject. Also, check with your local quilt shop for hand-quilting classes. As with anything, practice makes perfect!

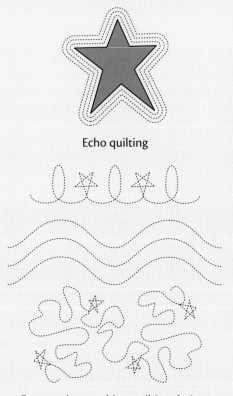

Echo quilting

Free-motion machine-quilting designs

BINDING

Once the quilt is quilted, you'll need to bind it. Single-fold binding is used when a quilt is handled or laundered rarely, such as wall hangings and table runners. Double-fold binding is better for quilts that will be handled or laundered regularly, such as lap and bed quilts. The strips used are generally cut on the crosswise grain (width of fabric). Bias strips can be used but are not necessary for the straight edges of the projects in this book. Follow these steps for double-fold binding.

1. Cut the strips the width indicated in the project instructions. Lay the strips perpendicular to each other and draw a line from the point where the strips meet at the upper left to where the strips meet at the lower right. Stitch on the drawn line. Trim ¼" from the stitching. Press the seam allowances open.

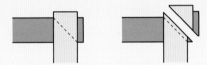

2. Trim the starting end of the binding at a 45° angle and press under a narrow hem to finish the raw edge.

3. Press the strip in half lengthwise, wrong sides together.

Fold line

4. With raw edges aligned, pin the binding to the quilt top, placing the first pin 2" from the beginning of the strip and the last pin ¼" from the corner. Begin sewing at the first pin and end

sewing at the last pin; backstitch. Remove the quilt from the machine.

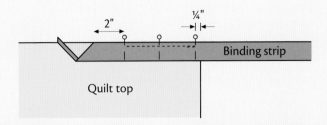

2"   ¼"

Binding strip

Quilt top

5. Rotate the quilt so you are ready to sew the next edge. Fold the binding up so that the fold makes a 45° angle, and then fold it back down onto itself so the raw edges are aligned. Pin the binding in place as before, placing the last pin ¼" from the next corner. Begin stitching at the edge, backstitch, and then continue stitching until you reach the last pin; backstitch. Repeat to sew the remaining corners.

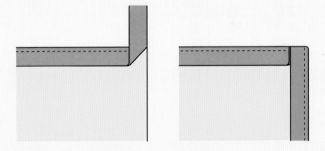

6. When you're close to the beginning of the binding, trim the end of the strip so that it overlaps the beginning tail about 1½". Tuck the end of the binding into the beginning of the binding and finish sewing the binding to the quilt.

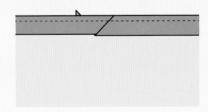

7. Fold the binding to the back of the quilt and hand blindstitch the folded edge in place with matching-colored thread, mitering the corners.

Star of Freedom

Finished Quilt Size: 28" x 28" • Finished Block Size: 12" x 12"

Materials

Yardages are based on 42"-wide fabric. Fat quarters measure 18" x 21" and fat eighths measure 9" x 21".

4 fat quarters of assorted tan fabrics for star blocks and border

1 fat quarter of dark brown fabric for star blocks

2 fat eighths of assorted dark brown fabrics for star blocks

2 fat eighths of assorted dark blue fabrics for star blocks

2 fat eighths of assorted medium purple fabrics for star blocks

2 fat eighths of assorted medium blue fabrics for star blocks

1 fat eighth of medium green 1 fabric for stems and leaves

10" x 10" square of medium red fabric for flower

6" x 12" rectangle of medium green 2 fabric for calyxes

5" x 5" square of medium gold fabric for flower center

4" x 4" square of dark purple fabric for medallion

2" x 2" square of dark red fabric for medallion center

1 fat quarter of dark blue fabric for binding

1⅛ yards of backing fabric

36" x 36" piece of batting

Cutting

Cut strips across the width of the fabric unless instructed otherwise. Although the four blocks are the same pattern, there are two different color placements, represented in the cutting instructions as block 1 and block 2. When cutting your fabrics, keep the pieces for blocks 1 and 2 separate. Before you begin cutting, set aside one tan fat quarter for the border.

BLOCK 1

From 3 of the tan fat quarters, cut a total of:
- ✦ 2 squares, 4½" x 4½"
- ✦ 8 squares, 2⅞" x 2⅞"
- ✦ 32 squares, 2½" x 2½"

From 1 assorted dark blue fat eighth, cut:
- ✦ 8 rectangles, 2½" x 4½"

From the dark brown fat quarter, cut:
- ✦ 8 rectangles, 2½" x 4½"

From 1 assorted dark brown fat eighth, cut:
- ✦ 8 squares, 2½" x 2½"

From 1 assorted medium purple fat eighth, cut:
- ✦ 8 squares, 2⅞" x 2⅞"

From 1 assorted medium blue fat eighth, cut:
- ✦ 8 squares, 2½" x 2½"

BLOCK 2

From 3 of the tan fat quarters, cut a total of:
- ✦ 2 squares, 4½" x 4½"
- ✦ 8 squares, 2⅞" x 2⅞"
- ✦ 24 squares, 2½" x 2½"

From the dark brown fat quarter, cut:
- ✦ 8 rectangles, 2½" x 4½"

From 1 assorted dark brown fat eighth, cut:
- ✦ 8 squares, 2½" x 2½"

From 1 assorted medium purple fat eighth, cut:
- ✦ 16 squares, 2½" x 2½"

From 1 assorted dark blue fat eighth, cut:
- ✦ 8 rectangles, 2½" x 4½"

From 1 assorted medium blue fat eighth, cut:
- ✦ 8 squares, 2⅞" x 2⅞"

BORDER AND BINDING

From the remaining tan fat quarter, cut:
- ✦ 4 strips, 2¼" x 14¼"*
- ✦ 4 strips, 2¼" x 12½"*

*Make all cuts across the 21" width of your fat quarter.

From the dark blue fat quarter for binding, cut:
- ✦ 7 strips, 2" x 21"

This project can be an attractive wall hanging or table topper. The four blocks that make up this quilt are actually the same. Creative use of color and value makes them look like two different blocks. In the general quiltmaking section of this book, you'll find helpful tips on picking fabrics to make a scrappy quilt.

Making Block 1

After sewing each seam, press the seam allowances in the direction indicated by the arrows (or press them open).

1. Refer to "Folded-Corner Technique" on page 8. Draw a diagonal line from corner to corner on the wrong side of the tan 2½" squares. Lay a marked square on one end of a dark blue rectangle, right sides together, as shown. Sew along the line, trim, and press the resulting triangle open. In the same manner, sew a marked square on the other end of the rectangle to make a flying-geese unit. Make a total of eight dark blue/tan flying-geese units.

Make 8.

2. Repeat step 1 using the remaining marked tan squares and the dark brown rectangles to make a total of eight dark brown/tan flying-geese units.

Make 8.

3. Refer to "Triangle Squares" on page 7. Use the tan 2⅞" squares and the medium purple squares to make 16 triangle squares as shown.

Make 16.

4. Lay out one medium blue 2½" square, one dark brown 2½" square, and two triangle squares from step 3 as shown. Sew the squares together in rows, and then sew the rows together to make a unit. The unit should measure 4½" square. Make eight units.

Make 8.

5. Sew a dark blue/tan flying-geese unit to each dark brown/tan flying-geese unit as shown to make a unit. The unit should measure 4½" square. Make eight.

Make 8.

6. Sew units from step 4 to opposite sides of a unit from step 5 to make a row, making sure to position the units exactly as shown. Make four.

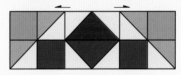

Make 4.

7. Sew units from step 5 to opposite sides of a tan 4½" square, making sure to rotate the units as shown. Make two of these rows.

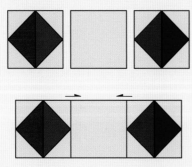

Make 2.

8. Sew two rows from step 6 to a row from step 7 as shown to complete block 1. Make two of block 1.

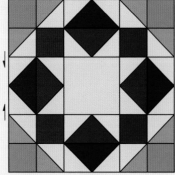

Block 1.
Make 2.

Making Block 2

1. Refer to step 1 of "Making Block 1." Use 16 tan 2½" squares and the dark brown rectangles to make eight dark brown/tan flying-geese units. Use the medium purple squares and the dark blue rectangles to make eight dark blue/medium purple flying-geese units.

2. Refer to "Triangle Squares" on page 7. Using the 2⅞" tan squares and the medium blue squares, make 16 triangle squares.

3. Lay out one tan 2½" square, one dark brown 2½" square, and two triangle squares from step 2 as shown. Sew the squares together in rows, and then sew the rows together to make a unit. The unit should measure 4½" square. Make eight units.

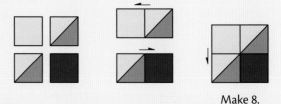

Make 8.

4. Sew a dark blue/medium purple flying-geese unit to each dark brown/tan flying-geese unit as shown to make a unit. The unit should measure 4½" square. Make eight.

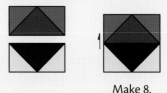

Make 8.

5. Sew units from step 3 to opposite sides of a unit from step 4 to make a row, making sure to position the units exactly as shown. Make four.

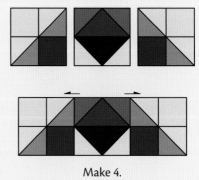

Make 4.

6. Sew units from step 4 to opposite sides of a tan 4½" square, making sure to rotate the units as shown. Make two of these rows.

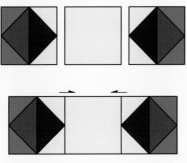

Make 2.

7. Sew two rows from step 5 to a row from step 6 as shown to complete block 2. Make two of block 2.

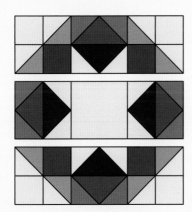

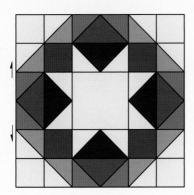

Block 2.
Make 2.

Assembling the Quilt Top

1. Lay out blocks 1 and 2 in two rows of two blocks each, rotating the blocks as shown. Sew the blocks together in rows, and then sew the rows together.

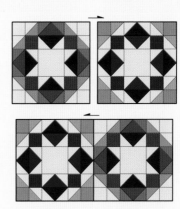

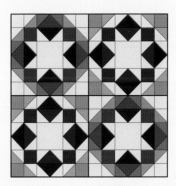

2. Join the tan 2¼" x 12½" strips in pairs along the short ends to make two 24½"-long border strips. Join the 2¼" x 14¼" strips in pairs along the short ends to make two 28"-long border strips.

3. Sew the border strips to the sides of the quilt top, and then the top and bottom.

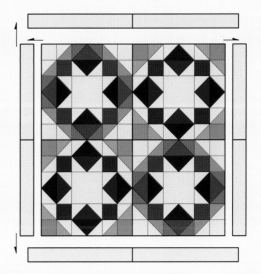

Adding the Appliqué

Use your preferred method of appliqué or refer to "Appliqué" on page 9 for more information on needle-turn hand appliqué and fusible-web machine appliqué. Refer to the diagram below for appliqué placement.

1. From medium green 1 fabric, cut four 1" x 9" bias strips. Refer to "Making Bias Stems" on page 10 to make stems from the bias strips. Appliqué the stems in place. The flower and medallion appliqués will cover the stem raw ends.

2. Using the patterns on page 21 and your preferred method, make the appliqué shapes from the fabrics indicated.

3. Appliqué the shapes in place, working in numerical order.

Appliqué placement

Finishing the Quilt

Refer to "Finishing Techniques" on page 12 for instructions as needed.

1. Layer the quilt top with batting and backing; baste.

2. Quilt as desired. I machine quilted my quilt with an overall meandering stitch that also included stars. I echo quilted inside the stems, flowers, and leaves to make them stand out.

3. Use the dark blue 2"-wide strips to bind the quilt.

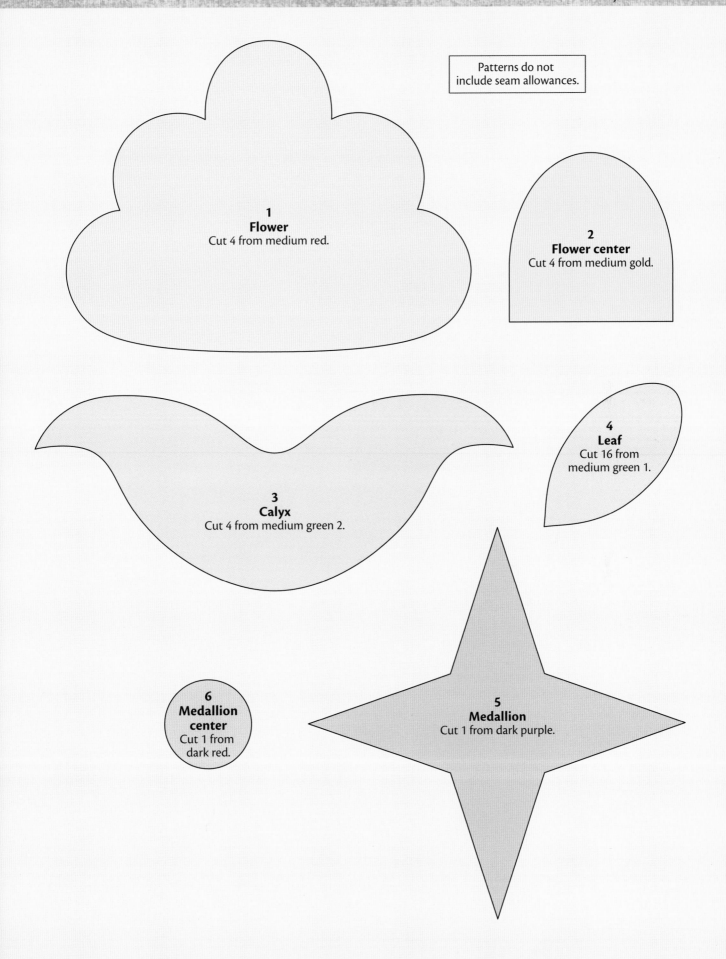

Patterns do not include seam allowances.

1
Flower
Cut 4 from medium red.

2
Flower center
Cut 4 from medium gold.

3
Calyx
Cut 4 from medium green 2.

4
Leaf
Cut 16 from medium green 1.

6
Medallion center
Cut 1 from dark red.

5
Medallion
Cut 1 from dark purple.

Blooming Stars

Finished Quilt Size: 62" x 62" • **Finished Block Size:** 14" x 14"

Quilted by Annette Ashbach of The Quiltmaker's Nest

Materials

Yardages are based on 42"-wide fabric. Fat quarters measure 18" x 21".

23 strips, 2½" x 42", OR ½ yard *each* of 4 assorted medium fabrics for blocks*

13 fat quarters OR 2⅞ yards *total* of assorted tan fabrics for blocks

6 fat quarters OR 1¼ yards *total* of assorted brown fabrics for blocks

1 yard of medium blue fabric for border

½ yard of medium red fabric for binding

3¾ yards of backing fabric

70" x 70" piece of batting

Cut each ½ yard of fabric into six 2½" x 42" strips (1 is extra).

Cutting

Cut strips across the width of the fabric. The pieces in this block are labeled A through G. When cutting pieces for the blocks, you'll want to cut the amount needed from various fabrics to achieve the desired scrappy look. For example, you would not want to cut all of the A pieces from the same strips of fabric.

From the assorted medium fabrics, cut a total of:
✦ 64 rectangles, 2½" x 6½" (E)
✦ 64 rectangles, 2½" x 4½" (A)
✦ 64 squares, 2½" x 2½" (B)

From the assorted tan fabrics, cut a total of:
✦ 64 squares, 4½" x 4½" (F)
✦ 64 rectangles, 2½" x 4½" (D)
✦ 208 squares, 2½" x 2½" (C)

From the assorted brown fabrics, cut:
✦ 64 squares, 4½" x 4½" (G)

From the medium blue border fabric, cut:
✦ 8 strips, 3¼" x 42"

From the medium red binding fabric, cut:
✦ 7 strips, 2" x 42"

Making the Blooming Star Blocks

Refer to "Folded-Corner Technique" on page 8 as needed. After sewing each seam, press the seam allowances in the direction indicated by the arrows (or press them open).

1. Draw a diagonal line from corner to corner on the wrong side of 128 tan C squares. With right sides together, place a marked square on one end of a medium E rectangle, making sure the drawn line is positioned as shown. Sew along the marked line and trim the excess fabric, leaving a ¼" seam allowance. Make a total of 64 E/C units.

Make 64.

2. Place a marked C square from step 1 on one end of a medium A rectangle, right sides together, with the drawn line positioned as shown. Sew along the line and trim the excess fabric, leaving a ¼" seam allowance. Make a total of 64 A/C units.

Make 64.

3. Draw a diagonal line from corner to corner on the wrong side of the medium B squares. Place a marked B square on one end of a tan D rectangle, right sides together, with the drawn line positioned as shown. Sew along the line and trim the excess fabric, leaving a ¼" seam allowance. Make a total of 64 D/B units.

Make 64.

This lap quilt is perfect for all those great precut 2¹/₂"-wide strips we all have! If you do not have any precut strips, buy pieces of fabric, ¹/₄ yard or larger, in a wide assortment of your favorite colors and cut them into 2¹/₂"-wide strips. You'll need at least a total of two yards of fabric. You can use as few or as many different fabric strips as you want.

4. Join a tan C square to the top of an A/C unit as shown. Make 64.

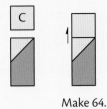

Make 64.

5. Join a tan F square to a D/B unit, making sure to position the D/B unit as shown. Make 64.

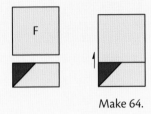

Make 64.

6. Join a unit from step 4 to a unit from step 5 as shown to make a corner unit. The unit should measure 6½" square. Make a total of 64 units.

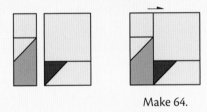

Make 64.

7. Sew two corner units from step 6 to opposite sides of an E/C unit as shown, rotating the corner units as needed so that the star points are pointing away from the E/C unit. Make 32.

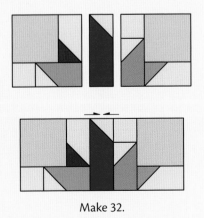

Make 32.

8. Sew E/C units to opposite sides of a tan C square as shown. Make 16.

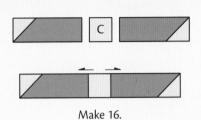

Make 16.

9. Lay out two units from step 7 and one unit from step 8, making sure the units are facing in the direction shown. Sew the units together to make a block. The block should measure 14½" square. Make 16 blocks.

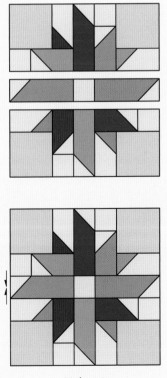

Make 16.

10. Draw a diagonal line from corner to corner on the wrong side of the brown G squares. Place a marked square on the upper-right corner of a block as shown, right sides together. Sew along the line and trim the excess fabric, leaving a ¼" seam allowance. Repeat, adding a brown square to the remaining three corners of the block. Make a total of 16 Blooming Star blocks.

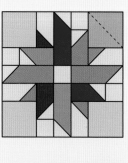
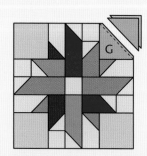

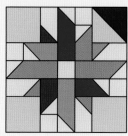

Make 16.

Assembling the Quilt Top

1. Lay out the Blooming Star blocks in four rows of four blocks each. Sew the blocks together into rows, and then sew the rows together to complete the quilt top.

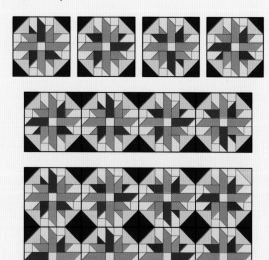

2. Refer to "Border Strips" on page 11. Measure the length of your quilt top; it should be 56½". Trim four of the medium blue strips to 28½" long. Join the strips in pairs along the short ends to make two 56½"-long strips and sew them to the sides of the quilt top.

3. Measure the width of your quilt top (including the just-added borders); it should be 62". Trim the remaining medium blue strips to 31¼" long. Join the strips in pairs along the short ends to make two 62"-long strips and sew them to the top and bottom of the quilt top.

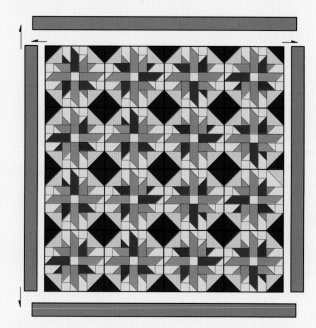

Finishing the Quilt

Refer to "Finishing Techniques" on page 12 for instructions as needed.

1. Layer the quilt top with batting and backing; baste.

2. Quilt as desired. This quilt was professionally machine quilted by a long-arm quilter. She quilted an overall meandering stitch that included stars.

3. Use the 2"-wide medium red strips to bind the quilt.

Star Trellis

Finished Quilt Size: 66" x 66" · Finished Block Size: 12" x 12"

Quilted by Annette Ashbach of The Quiltmaker's Nest

Materials

Yardages are based on 42"-wide fabric. Fat quarters measure 18" x 21" and fat eighths measure 9" x 21".

⅞ yard *each* of 2 assorted tan fabrics for setting blocks

½ yard *each* of 2 assorted medium green 1 fabrics for stem, leaf, and calyx appliqués

4 fat quarters of assorted dark gold or medium brown fabrics for setting blocks

3 fat quarters of assorted medium tan fabrics for Twisted Star blocks

3 fat quarters of assorted light tan fabrics for Twisted Star blocks

3 fat quarters of assorted medium green 2 fabrics for Twisted Star blocks

2 fat quarters of assorted dark red 1 fabrics for Twisted Star blocks

2 fat quarters of assorted medium gold fabrics for Twisted Star blocks

4 fat eighths of assorted medium/dark blue fabrics for Twisted Star blocks

1 fat quarter of dark red 2 fabric for center flower appliqués

1 fat quarter of dark purple fabric for outer flower appliqués

1 fat eighth of dark blue fabric for center flower appliqués

8" x 10" rectangle of medium gold fabric for center flower appliqués

⅞ yard of dark blue fabric for border

½ yard of dark red fabric for binding

4½ yards of backing fabric

74" x 74" piece of batting

Cutting

Cut strips across the width of the fabric unless instructed otherwise. Refer to "Making Bias Stems" on page 10 for instructions on cutting bias strips.

From the fat quarters of assorted dark red 1 fabrics, cut a total of:
+ 13 squares, 5¼" x 5¼"; cut the squares into quarters diagonally to yield 52 quarter-square triangles (C)

From the fat quarters of assorted medium gold fabrics, cut a total of:
+ 13 squares, 5¼" x 5¼"; cut the squares into quarters diagonally to yield 52 quarter-square triangles (D)

From the fat quarters of assorted medium green 2 fabrics, cut:
+ 26 squares, 4⅞" x 4⅞"; cut the squares in half diagonally to yield 52 half-square triangles (B)

From the fat quarters of assorted medium tan fabrics, cut a total of:
+ 26 squares, 4½" x 4½" (E)

From the fat quarters of assorted light tan fabrics, cut a total of:
+ 26 squares, 4½" x 4½" (E)

From the fat eighths of assorted medium/dark blue fabrics, cut a total of:
+ 13 squares, 4½" x 4½" (A)

From *each* ⅞ yard of assorted tan fabrics, cut:
+ 6 squares, 12½" x 12½" (12 total; F)

From the fat quarters of assorted dark gold or medium brown fabrics, cut a total of:
+ 48 squares, 4½" x 4½" (G)

From the dark blue border fabric, cut:
+ 8 strips, 3¼" x 42"

From 1 medium green 1 fabric, cut:
+ 12 bias strips, 1" x 13"
+ Reserve the remaining fabric for the leaf and calyx appliqués.

From the dark red binding fabric, cut:
+ 7 strips, 2" x 42"

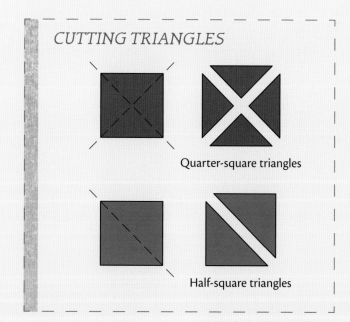

CUTTING TRIANGLES

Quarter-square triangles

Half-square triangles

Flowers climb a trellis of stars in this fun lap quilt. I concentrated on using four main colors in this quilt: red, green, gold, and blue. I used several different fabrics in these main colors to achieve a scrappy look. Feel free to substitute your favorite colors to personalize the quilt.

Making the Twisted Star Blocks

After sewing each seam, press the seam allowances in the direction indicated by the arrows (or press them open).

1. Join the dark red C triangles to the medium gold D triangles as shown. Make 52 units.

Make 52.

2. Join C/D units to medium green B triangles to make 52 units. The units should measure 4½" square.

Make 52.

3. Join medium tan and light tan E squares to opposite sides of a unit from step 2 as shown. Make 26.

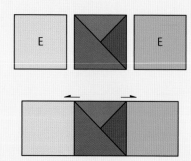

Make 26.

4. Join units from step 2 to opposite sides of a medium/dark blue A square as shown. Make 13.

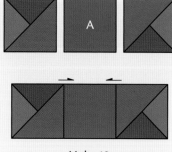

Make 13.

5. Lay out two units from step 3 and one unit from step 4 as shown. Sew the units together to complete a Twisted Star block. The block should measure 12½" square. Make 13 blocks.

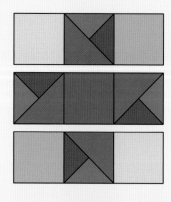

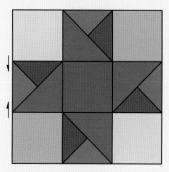

Make 13.

Making the Setting Blocks

After sewing each seam, press the seam allowances in the direction indicated by the arrows (or press them open).

1. Refer to "Folded-Corner Technique" on page 8. Draw a diagonal line from corner to corner on the wrong side of each dark gold/medium brown G square. Place a marked square on the upper-right corner of an F square, right sides together. Sew along the line and trim the excess fabric, leaving a ¼" seam allowance. Repeat on the opposite corner of the F square.

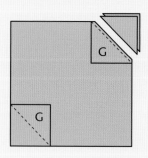 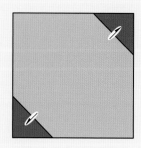

Make 12.

2. Repeat step 1, sewing G squares to the remaining two corners of each F square to complete 12 setting blocks.

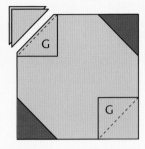 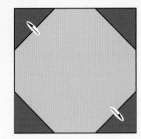

Make 12.

Adding the Appliqué

At this point, you'll appliqué the stems, center leaf, and flower in the center of the setting blocks. Use your preferred method of appliqué or refer to "Appliqué" on page 9 for more information on needle-turn hand appliqué and fusible-web machine appliqué. Refer to the diagram for appliqué placement.

1. Refer to "Making Bias Stems" on page 10 to make stems from the medium green bias strips. Appliqué them in place. The outer flower and outer flower calyx appliqués will cover the raw ends of the stems.

2. Using the patterns on pages 32 and 33 and your preferred method of appliqué, make the appliqué shapes from the designated fabric.

3. Appliqué the center leaf (1) and flower pieces (2, 3, and 4) in the center of the setting blocks, working in numerical order. (The outer flowers and calyxes will be appliquéd in place after the borders are attached to the quilt top.)

Appliqué placement

Assembling the Quilt Top

1. Join three Twisted Star blocks and two setting blocks, alternating them as shown to make a row. Make three of these rows.

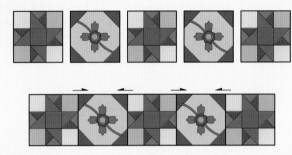

Make 3.

2. Join three setting blocks and two Twisted Star blocks, alternating them as shown to make a row. Make two of these rows.

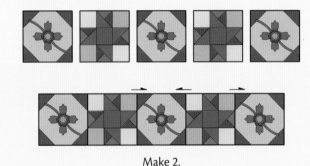

Make 2.

3. Lay out the rows as shown. Sew the rows together and press the seam allowances in one direction (or press them open).

4. Refer to "Border Strips" on page 11. Measure the length of your quilt top; it should be 60½". Trim four of the dark blue strips to 30½" long. Join the strips in pairs along the short ends to make two 60½"-long strips and sew them to the sides of the quilt top.

5. Measure the width of your quilt top (including the just-added borders); it should be 66". Trim the remaining dark blue strips to 33¼" long. Join the strips in pairs along the short ends to make two 66"-long strips and sew them to the top and bottom of the quilt top.

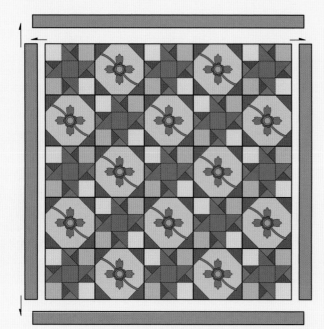

6. Appliqué the outer flowers and calyxes to the quilt top as shown in the photo. Note that the appliqués overlap the side borders.

Finishing the Quilt

Refer to "Finishing Techniques" on page 12 for instructions as needed.

1. Layer the quilt top with batting and backing; baste.

2. Quilt as desired. This quilt was professionally machine quilted by a long-arm quilter. She quilted an overall meandering stitch that included stars. The stems, flowers, and leaves are echo quilted to make them stand out.

3. Use the dark red 2"-wide strips to bind the quilt.

> Patterns do not
> include seam allowances.

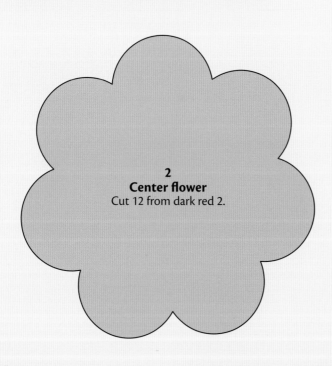

2
Center flower
Cut 12 from dark red 2.

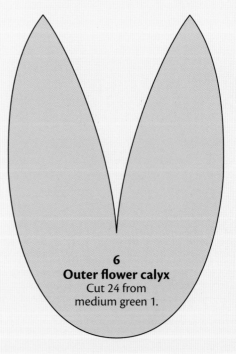

6
Outer flower calyx
Cut 24 from
medium green 1.

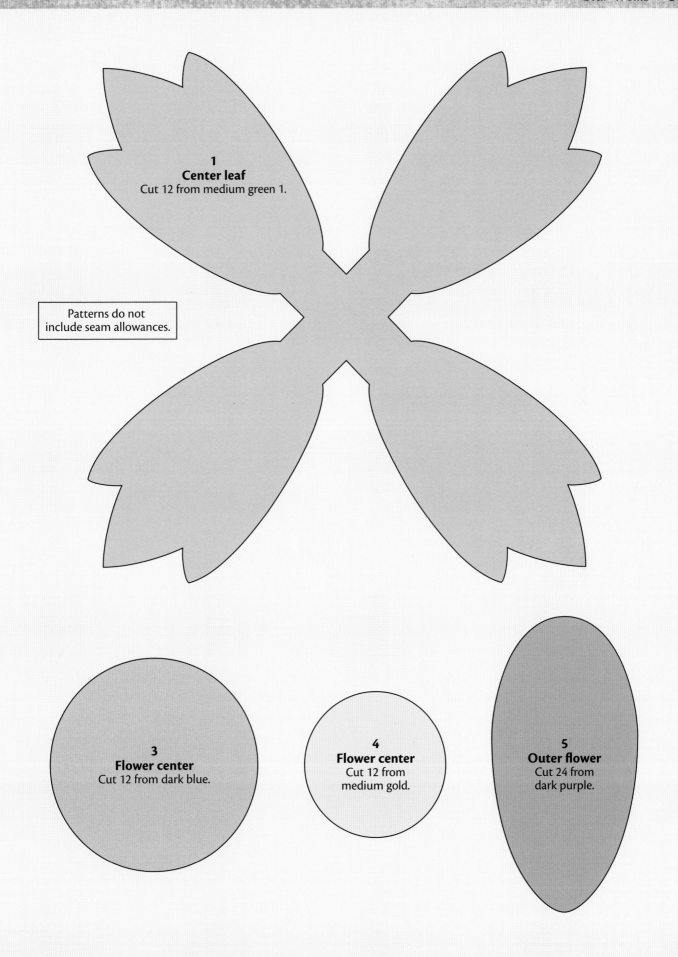

1
Center leaf
Cut 12 from medium green 1.

Patterns do not
include seam allowances.

3
Flower center
Cut 12 from dark blue.

4
Flower center
Cut 12 from
medium gold.

5
Outer flower
Cut 24 from
dark purple.

Checkerboard Stars

Finished Quilt Size: 65⅜" x 65⅜" • **Finished Block Size:** 11⅞" x 11⅞"

Quilted by Mindy Prohaski of Quilting on Cameo

Materials

Yardages are based on 42"-wide fabric. Fat quarters measure 18" x 21".

12 fat quarters of assorted light fabrics for blocks

10 fat quarters of assorted dark fabrics for blocks

6 fat quarters of assorted medium fabrics for blocks

1⅛ yards of light fabric for borders

½ yard of dark fabric for binding

4½ yards of backing fabric

74" x 74" piece of batting

BEFORE YOU CUT

Before you begin cutting, select four light fat quarters and five dark fat quarters for setting triangles. These triangles are used to set the Star blocks on point.

   In block 1 the pieces are labeled A through D. In block 2 they are labeled A through E. When cutting a particular piece, you'll want to cut the amount needed from various fat quarters to achieve the desired scrappy look. For example, you would not want to cut all of the A pieces from the same fat quarter. Careful planning will help you determine how many of each piece to cut from a specific fat quarter. A handy tip is to draw the quilt top on graph paper and then use colored pencils to attain the desired color placement. Be sure to label all your pieces with the block number and letter!

Cutting

Cut strips across the width of the fabric. When cutting your fabrics, keep the pieces for blocks 1 and 2 separate.

BLOCK 1

From 8 of the assorted light fat quarters, cut a total of:

✦ 52 rectangles, 2½" x 4½" (C)

✦ 104 squares, 2½" x 2½" (B)

From the assorted medium fat quarters, cut a total of:

✦ 13 squares, 4½" x 4½" (A)

From 5 of the assorted dark fat quarters, cut a total of:

✦ 104 squares, 2½" x 2½" (D)

BLOCK 2

From 8 of the assorted light fat quarters, cut a total of:

✦ 12 squares, 4½" x 4½" (A)

✦ 96 squares, 2½" x 2½" (D)

From the assorted medium fat quarters, cut a total of:

✦ 48 rectangles, 2½" x 4½" (C)

✦ 48 squares, 2½" x 2½" (E)

From 5 of the assorted dark fat quarters, cut a total of:

✦ 48 squares, 2½" x 2½" (B)

SETTING TRIANGLES

From 4 of the assorted light fat quarters, cut a total of:

✦ 24 squares, 6⅝" x 6⅝"; cut the squares in half diagonally to yield 48 half-square triangles

From 5 of the assorted dark fat quarters, cut a total of:

✦ 26 squares, 6⅝" x 6⅝"; cut the squares in half diagonally to yield 52 half-square triangles

BORDERS AND BINDING

From the light border fabric, cut:

✦ 8 strips, 4½" x 42"

From the remaining assorted dark fabrics, cut a total of:

✦ 4 squares, 4½" x 4½"

From the remaining assorted light fabrics, cut a total of:

✦ 16 squares, 2½" x 2½"

From the dark binding fabric, cut:

✦ 7 strips, 2" x 42"

This quilt presents a great opportunity to play with many colors. You'll be using a total of 28 fat quarters. Have fun with the color combinations! Since the top is made of just one kind of block, set on point, the color is what makes this quilt sing.

Making Block 1

Refer to "Folded-Corner Technique" on page 8. After sewing each seam, press the seam allowances in the direction indicated by the arrows (or press them open).

1. Draw a diagonal line from corner to corner on the wrong side of 52 of the light B squares. Place a marked square on the upper-right corner of a medium A square as shown, right sides together. Sew along the line and trim the excess fabric, leaving a ¼" seam allowance.

2. Repeat step 1, adding marked squares to the remaining three corners of the A square to make a center unit. The unit should measure 4½" square. Make 13 units.

Make 13.

3. Using the folded-corner technique, join two dark D squares to one light C rectangle to make a flying-geese unit. Make 52 units.

Make 52.

4. Join a light B square to opposite ends of a flying-geese unit from step 3 to make a row. Make 26.

Make 26.

5. Join flying-geese units from step 3 to opposite sides of a center unit from step 2 as shown to make a row. Make 13.

Make 13.

6. Lay out two rows from step 4 and one row from step 5 as shown. Join the rows to complete the block. The block should measure 8½" square. Make 13 blocks.

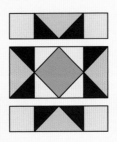 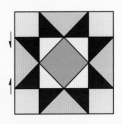

Make 13.

Making Block 2

After sewing each seam, press the seam allowances in the direction indicated by the arrows (or press them open).

1. Draw a diagonal line from corner to corner on the wrong side of the dark B squares. Using the marked squares and the light A squares, repeat steps 1 and 2 in "Making Block 1" to make 12 center units.

Make 12.

2. Using the folded-corner technique, join two light D squares to one medium C rectangle to make a flying-geese unit. Make 48 units.

Make 48.

3. Join medium E squares to opposite ends of a flying-geese unit from step 2 to make a row. Make 24.

   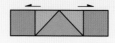

Make 24.

4. Join flying-geese units from step 2 to opposite sides of a center unit from step 1 to make a row. Make 12.

   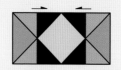

Make 12.

5. Lay out two rows from step 3 and one row from step 4 as shown. Join the rows to complete the block. The block should measure 8½" square. Make 12 blocks.

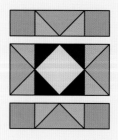 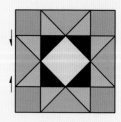

Make 12.

Adding the Setting Triangles

After sewing each seam, press the seam allowances in the direction indicated by the arrows (or press them open).

1. Join dark half-square triangles to opposite sides of each block 1, making sure the triangles are centered along the sides of the block. The ends of the triangles will extend beyond the block a little; *do not* trim off these ends after sewing. Take care when pressing the bias edge of the triangles as it can easily be stretched.

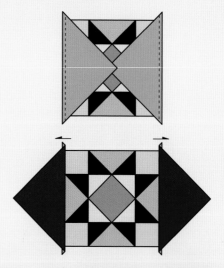

2. Repeat step 1, sewing dark triangles to the remaining two sides of each block 1. Make 13.

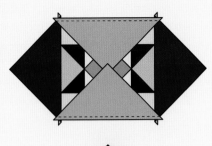

Make 13.

3. Repeat steps 1 and 2, sewing light half-square triangles to each block 2. Make 12.

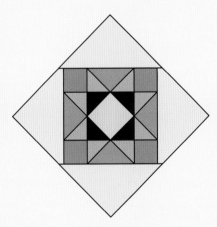

Make 12.

4. Trim and square up the blocks, making sure to leave ¼" beyond the points of the Star blocks for seam allowance. The blocks should all be the same size.

Assembling the Quilt Top

1. Lay out three of block 1 and two of block 2, alternating them as shown. Join the blocks to make a row. Press the seam allowances in one direction (or press them open). Make three of these rows.

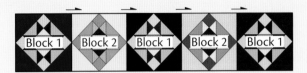

Make 3.

2. Lay out three of block 2 and two of block 1, alternating them as shown. Join the blocks to make a row. Press the seam allowances in one direction (or press them open). Make two of these rows.

Make 2.

3. Lay out the rows, alternating them as shown. Join the rows and press the seam allowances in one direction (or press them open).

Adding the Borders

1. Draw a diagonal line from corner to corner on the wrong side of the light 2½" border squares. Using the marked squares and the dark 4½" border squares, repeat steps 1 and 2 in "Making Block 1" to make four corner units. Each unit should measure 4½" square.

Make 4.

2. Refer to "Border Strips" on page 11. Measure the length and width of your quilt top; it should measure 57⅜". Trim four of the light border strips to measure 29" long. Trim the remaining four light border strips to 28⅞". Join a 29"-long strip and a 28⅞"-long strip along the short ends to make a 57⅜"-long strip. Make four of these border strips.

3. Join a border strip to opposite sides of the quilt top. Join a corner unit from step 1 to the ends of the remaining two border strips. Sew the strips to the top and bottom of the quilt top. Press the seam allowances toward the strips.

Finishing the Quilt

Refer to "Finishing Techniques" on page 12 for instructions as needed.

1. Layer the quilt top with batting and backing; baste.

2. Quilt as desired. This quilt was professionally machine quilted by a long-arm quilter. She quilted an overall meandering pattern that included stars.

3. Use the dark 2"-wide strips to bind the quilt.

Star Wheels

Finished Quilt Size: 72½" x 72½" • **Finished Block Size:** 12" x 12"

Quilted by Mindy Prohaski of Quilting on Cameo

Materials

Yardages are based on 42"-wide fabric. Fat quarters measure 18" x 21".

27 strips, 2½" x 42", OR ¼ yard of 9 assorted dark fabrics for blocks*

27 strips, 2½" x 42", OR ¼ yard of 9 assorted medium fabrics for blocks*

7 fat quarters of assorted tan 1 fabrics for blocks

6 fat quarters OR 1⅛ yards of assorted black 1 fabrics for outer border

5 fat quarters OR 1¼ yards of assorted tan 2 fabrics for outer border

4 fat quarters of assorted black 3 fabrics for appliquéd circles

⅔ yard of black 2 fabric for inner border

2 fat quarters of assorted gold for appliquéd stars

⅝ yard of medium or dark fabric for binding

4¾ yards of backing fabric

80" x 80" piece of batting

Cut each ¼ yard of fabric into three 2½" x 42" strips.

Cutting

Cut strips across the width of the fabric.

From the fat quarters of assorted tan 1 fabrics, cut a total of:
✦ 148 squares, 3½" x 3½"

From the black 2 fabric, cut:
✦ 4 strips, 2½" x 32½"
✦ 4 strips, 2½" x 30½"

From the fat quarters of assorted black 1 fabrics, cut a total of:
✦ 32 rectangles, 4½" x 8½"

From the fat quarters of assorted tan 2 fabrics, cut a total of:
✦ 68 squares, 4½" x 4½"

From the medium or dark binding fabric, cut:
✦ 8 strips, 2" x 42"

Making the Blocks

There are two different blocks: block 1 has circle and star appliqués, and block 2 is an alternating plain block. After sewing each seam, press the seam allowances in the direction indicated by the arrows (or press them open).

MAKING THE STRIP UNITS

1. Join 2½"-wide dark strips to both long sides of a 2½"-wide medium strip as shown to make strip set A. Make nine strip sets. Crosscut the strip sets into 50 segments, 6½" wide.

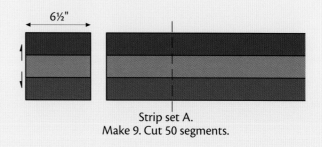

Strip set A.
Make 9. Cut 50 segments.

2. Join 2½"-wide medium strips to both long sides of a 2½"-wide dark strip as shown to make strip set B. Make nine of these strip sets. Crosscut the strip sets into 50 segments, 6½" wide.

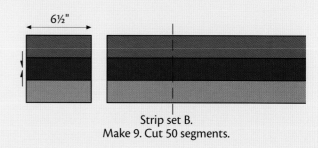

Strip set B.
Make 9. Cut 50 segments.

MAKING BLOCK 1

1. Lay out one A segment (with the strips vertical) and one B segment (with the strips horizontal) as shown. Join the segments to make a row. Make 26.

Make 26.

This lap quilt is a great for using all those precut 2¹/₂"-wide strip collections
you have accumulated in your stash. Or, you can just use regular yardage
and cut it into 2¹/₂"-wide strips. Like the "Blooming Stars" lap quilt on
page 22, you can use as few or as many different colors as you like.

2. Join two rows from step 1 to make a block, rotating one row as shown so that the A and B segments are opposite each other. The block should measure 12½" square. Make 13.

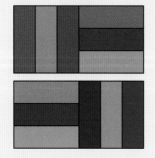 

Make 13.

3. Refer to "Folded-Corner Technique" on page 8. Draw a diagonal line from corner to corner on the wrong side of each 3½" tan square. Place a marked square on the upper-right corner of a block from step 2, right sides together. Sew along the line and trim the excess fabric, leaving a ¼" seam allowance.

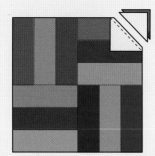 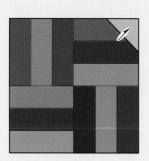

4. Repeat step 3, adding tan squares to the remaining three corners of the block. Make 13 blocks. Set aside the blocks for the appliqué section on page 45.

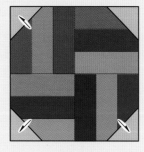

Make 13.

MAKING BLOCK 2

1. Repeating step 3 of "Making Block 1" and using the marked tan squares, place a marked square on the upper-left corner of an A segment as shown, right sides together. Sew along the line and trim. Repeat on the diagonally opposite corner of the A segment. Make 24 A units.

Unit A.
Make 24.

2. In the same manner as step 1, sew the remaining marked tan squares on diagonally opposite corners of each remaining B segment, making sure to place the tan squares as shown. Make 24 B units.

Unit B.
Make 24.

3. Lay out one A unit and one B unit as shown. Join the units to make a row. Make 24.

Make 24.

4. Join two rows from step 3 to make a block, rotating one row as shown so that the A and B units are opposite each other. Make 12 blocks.

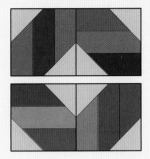 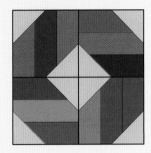

Make 12.

Adding the Appliqué

Use your preferred method of appliqué or refer to "Appliqué" on page 9 for more information on needle-turn hand appliqué and fusible-web machine appliqué. Refer to the diagram for appliqué placement.

1. Using the circle and star patterns on pages 47 and 48 and your preferred appliqué method, make the appliqué shapes from the fabrics indicated.

2. Appliqué the circle and then the star in the center of each block 1.

Appliqué placement

Assembling the Quilt Top

1. Join three of block 1 and two of block 2 to make a row, alternating them as shown. Press the seam allowances to one side (or press them open). Make three rows.

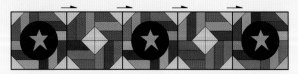

Make 3.

2. Join three of block 2 and two of block 1 to make a row, alternating them as shown. Press the seam allowances to one side (or press them open). Make two rows.

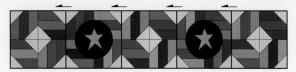

Make 2.

3. Lay out the rows as shown. Sew the rows together and press the seam allowances in one direction (or press them open). The quilt top should measure 60½" x 60½".

4. Refer to "Border Strips" on page 11 as needed. For the inner border, join two 2½" x 30½" black strips along the short ends to make a 60½"-long strip. Make two strips and sew them to the sides of the quilt top. Join two 2½" x 32½" black strips along the short ends to make a 64½"-long strip. Make two strips and sew them to the top and bottom of the quilt top. Press the seam allowances toward the strips.

Making the Outer Border

1. Draw a diagonal line from corner to corner on the wrong side of 64 tan 4½" squares. Using the marked squares and the black 4½" x 8½" rectangles, make 32 flying-geese units as shown, again referring to "Folded-Corner Technique" as needed.

Make 32.

2. Join eight flying-geese units to make a border strip as shown. Press the seam allowances open. Make four border strips.

Make 4.

3. Join border strips to opposite sides of the quilt top. Press the seam allowances toward the inner border. Join tan 4½" squares to the ends of the remaining two border strips. Press the seam allowances toward the tan squares, and then sew the borders to the top and bottom of the quilt top.

Finishing the Quilt

Refer to "Finishing Techniques" on page 12 for instructions as needed.

1. Layer the quilt top with batting and backing; baste.

2. Quilt as desired. This quilt was professionally machine quilted by a long-arm quilter. She quilted an overall meandering pattern that included stars. A large star was quilted inside each appliquéd star.

3. Use the medium or dark 2"-wide strips to bind the quilt.

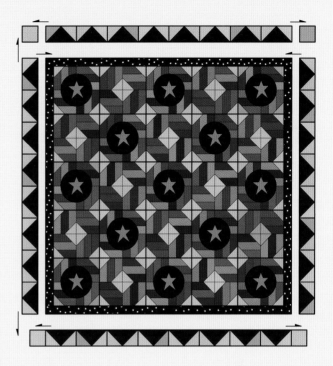

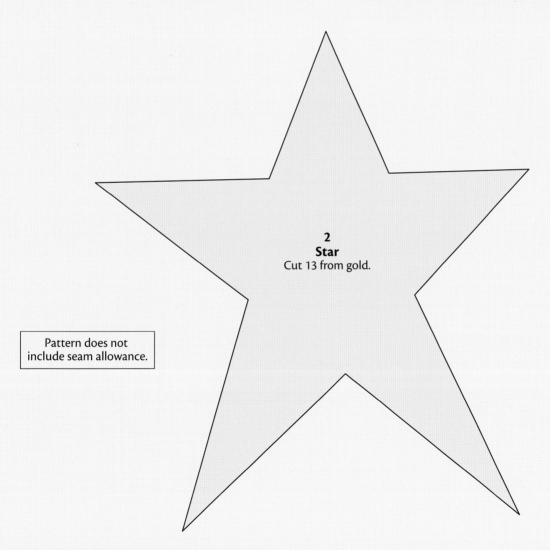

2
Star
Cut 13 from gold.

Pattern does not include seam allowance.

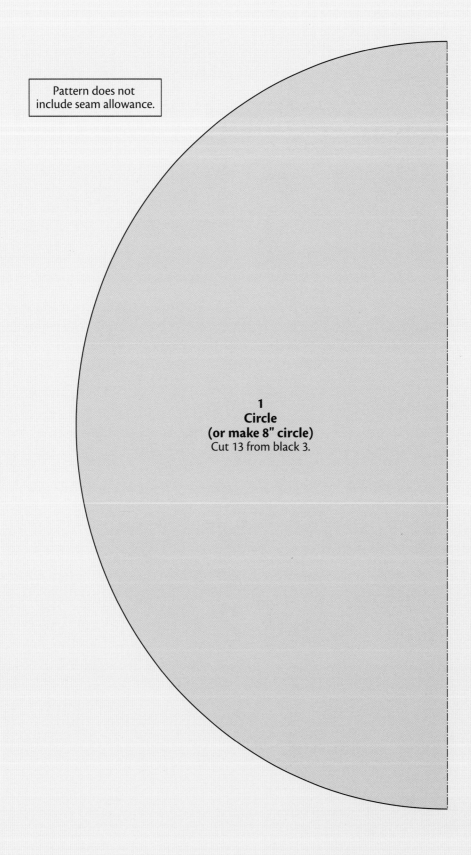

Pattern does not include seam allowance.

1
Circle
(or make 8" circle)
Cut 13 from black 3.

Star Chain

Finished Quilt Size: 74½" x 74½" • **Finished Block Size:** 14" x 14"

Quilted by Annette Ashbach of The Quiltmaker's Nest

Materials

Yardages are based on 42"-wide fabric. Fat quarters measure 18" x 21".

40 strips, 2½" x 42", OR ¼ yard of 14 assorted medium and dark fabrics for blocks*

17 strips, 2½" x 42", OR ¼ yard of 6 assorted light tan fabrics for blocks*

12 fat quarters of assorted dark tan fabrics for sashing and borders

3 fat quarters of assorted gold fabrics for sashing and borders

2 fat quarters of light tan fabric for sashing squares

⅝ yard of medium or dark blue for binding

5 yards of backing fabric

83" x 83" piece of batting

Cut each ¼ yard of fabric into 3 strips, 2½" x 42". You'll have 2 extra medium/dark strips and 1 extra light tan strip.

Cutting

Cut strips across the width of the fabric. Before cutting, set aside 7 medium/dark strips and 8 light tan strips to make the center nine-patch unit.

From 33 of the assorted medium or dark strips, cut a total of:
+ 64 strips, 2½" x 10½" (B)
+ 64 strips, 2½" x 6½" (A)

From 9 of the assorted light tan strips, cut a total of:
+ 128 squares, 2½" x 2½" (C)
+ 4 squares, 2" x 2" (I)

From the assorted dark tan fat quarters, cut a total of:
+ 40 strips, 3½" x 14½" (D)
+ 16 strips, 2" x 14½" (H)
+ 20 rectangles, 2" x 3½" (G)

From *each* of the assorted gold fat quarters, cut:
+ 68 squares, 2" x 2" (E; 204 total, 4 are extra)

From the light tan fat quarters, cut a total of:
+ 25 squares, 3½" x 3½" (F)

From the medium or dark blue binding fabric, cut:
+ 8 strips, 2" x 42"

Making the Nine-Patch Units

1. Join two light tan 2½" x 42" strips and one medium/ dark 2½" x 42" strip along their long edges as shown to make strip set A. Press the seam allowances toward the darker strip (or press them open). Make three. Crosscut the strip sets into 32 segments, 2½" wide.

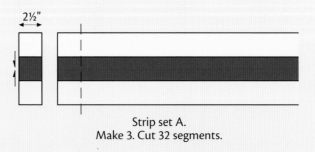

Strip set A.
Make 3. Cut 32 segments.

2. Join two medium/dark 2½" x 42" strips and one light tan 2½" x 42" strip along their long edges as shown to make strip set B. Press the seam allowances toward the darker strips (or press them open). Make two. Crosscut the strip sets into 16 segments, 2½" wide.

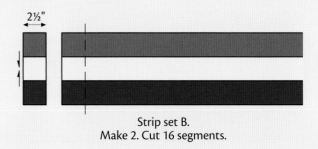

Strip set B.
Make 2. Cut 16 segments.

3. Lay out two A segments and one B segment as shown. Join the segments to make a nine-patch unit for the block center. Press the seam allowances toward the B segment (or press them open). Make 16 units, each measuring 6½" x 6½".

Make 16.

This lap quilt is another chance to use all of those precut 2½"-wide strips you've collected! It's made from one block, with clever sashing and border to make an overall "chain of stars" design. If you don't have precut strips, you can cut your own strips from yardage.

Making the Blocks

After sewing each seam, press the seam allowances in the direction indicated by the arrows (or press them open).

1. Join medium/dark A strips to opposite sides of a nine-patch unit as shown to make a row. Make 16 of these rows.

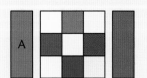 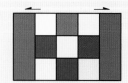

Make 16.

2. Join a light tan C square to both ends of each remaining A strip as shown to make a row. Make 32 rows.

Make 32.

3. Lay out two rows from step 2 and one row from step 1 as shown. Sew the rows together. Make 16.

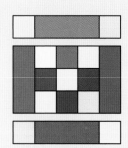 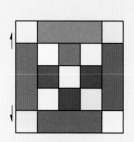

Make 16.

4. Join a medium/dark B strip to opposite sides of a unit from step 3 as shown to make a row. Make 16 rows.

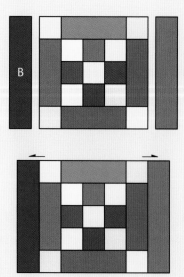

Make 16.

5. Join a light tan C square to both ends of each remaining B strip as shown to make a row. Make 32 rows.

Make 32.

6. Lay out two rows from step 5 and one row from step 4 as shown. Sew the rows together to complete a block. Make a total of 16 blocks. The blocks should measure 14½" x 14½".

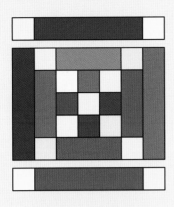

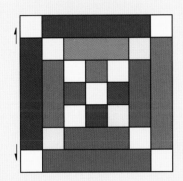

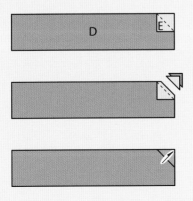

Make 16.

Making the Sashing and Border

Refer to "Folded-Corner Technique" on page 8. After sewing each seam, press the seam allowances in the direction indicated by the arrows (or press them open).

1. Draw a diagonal line from corner to corner on the wrong side of the gold E squares. Place a marked square on one corner of a dark tan D strip, right sides together. Sew along the line and trim the excess fabric, leaving a ¼" seam allowance. Press the resulting triangle open.

2. Repeat step 1, adding E squares to the remaining three corners of the D strip to make a sashing strip as shown. (I used two matching E squares on one end of the D strip and two different matching E squares on the other end.) Make 40 sashing strips.

Make 40.

3. Using the remaining E squares and the dark tan G rectangles, make 20 flying-geese units. Use matching E squares for each unit as shown. Set the units aside for step 1 of "Adding the Borders."

Make 20.

4. Lay out five light tan F squares and four sashing strips from step 2, starting and ending with an F square and alternating the pieces as shown. Sew the squares and sashing strips together to make a sashing row. Make five rows.

Make 5.

> ### GOLD STAR
> If you want your stars to have matching points like in my quilt on page 51, arrange your blocks, sashing strips, flying-geese units, and light tan F squares on a design wall. Then rearrange the pieces, rotating the sashing strips until the star points match. Once you are pleased with the arrangement, sew the pieces together into rows as instructed.

Assembling the Quilt Top

1. Lay out five sashing strips and four blocks, starting and ending with a sashing strip and alternating the pieces as shown. Sew the sashing strips and blocks together to make a block row. Press the seam allowances toward the blocks. Make four rows.

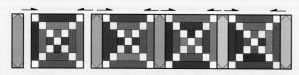

Make 4.

2. Lay out the sashing rows and block rows, starting and ending with a sashing row and alternating the rows as shown. Sew the rows together and press the seam allowances toward the sashing rows.

Adding the Border

1. Join five flying-geese units and four dark tan H strips to make a border strip as shown. Make four strips.

Make 4.

2. Join border strips to opposite sides of the quilt top. Then sew light tan I squares to the ends of the remaining two border strips and sew them to the top and bottom of the quilt top.

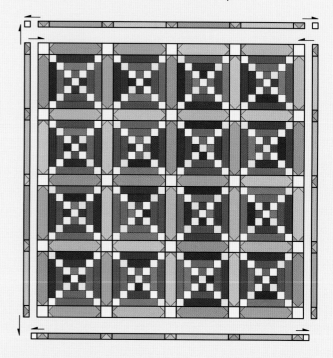

Finishing the Quilt

Refer to "Finishing Techniques" on page 12 for instructions as needed.

1. Layer the quilt top with batting and backing; baste.

2. Quilt as desired. This quilt was professionally machine quilted by a long-arm quilter. She quilted an overall meandering pattern that included stars.

3. Use the medium or dark blue 2"-wide strips to bind the quilt.

Scrappy Pinwheel Stars

Finished Quilt Size: 58" x 58" • **Finished Block Size:** 12" x 12"

Quilted by Mindy Prohaski of Quilting on Cameo

Materials

Yardages are based on 42"-wide fabric. Fat quarters measure 18" x 21" and fat eighths measure 9" x 21".

1⅞ yards of dark brown fabric for setting triangles and border

4 fat quarters of assorted light tan fabrics for blocks

4 fat quarters of assorted medium tan fabrics for blocks

2 fat quarters of assorted blue fabrics for blocks*

2 fat quarters of assorted red fabrics for blocks*

4 fat eighths of assorted brown fabrics for blocks

1 fat eighth *each* of red, blue, purple, and green fabrics for blocks

1 fat quarter of medium green fabric for stems and leaf appliqués

1 fat quarter of medium red fabric for flower appliqués

1 fat eighth of medium blue fabric for flower appliqués

8" x 8" square of gold fabric for flower appliqués

½ yard of blue fabric for binding

4 yards of backing fabric

66" x 66" of batting

Template plastic or cardstock

**For a scrappier look, use 4 fat eighths.*

Cutting

Cut strips across the width of the fabric unless instructed otherwise. Refer to "Cutting Triangles" on page 28 for instructions on cutting triangles. Refer to "Making Bias Stems" on page 10 for instructions on cutting bias strips.

From *each* of the red, blue, purple, and green fat eighths, cut:
- 2 strips, 3⅝" x 21" (8 total)

From 1 of the assorted light tan fat quarters, cut:
- 4 strips, 3⅝" x 21"

From the 3 remaining assorted light tan fat quarters, cut a total of:
- 14 squares, 3⅞" x 3⅞" (C)
- 28 rectangles, 2½" x 3" (H)
- 28 rectangles, 2" x 2½" (G)
- 28 rectangles, 1½" x 2½" (I)

From 1 of the assorted medium tan fat quarters, cut:
- 4 strips, 3⅝" x 21"

From the 3 remaining assorted medium tan fat quarters, cut a total of:
- 12 squares, 3⅞" x 3⅞" (C)
- 24 rectangles, 2½" x 3" (H)
- 24 rectangles, 2" x 2½" (G)
- 24 rectangles, 1½" x 2½" (I)

From the assorted brown fat eighths, cut a total of:
- 26 squares, 3⅞" x 3⅞" (D)

From the assorted blue fat quarters, cut a total of:
- 26 squares, 2½" x 2½" (J)
- 56 rectangles, 1½" x 2" (E)
- 24 squares, 1½" x 1½" (F)

From the assorted red fat quarters, cut a total of:
- 26 squares, 2½" x 2½" (J)
- 48 rectangles, 1½" x 2" (E)
- 28 squares, 1½" x 1½" (F)

From the dark brown fabric, cut:
- 8 strips, 3¾" x 42"
- 2 squares, 18¼" x 18¼"; cut the squares into quarters diagonally to yield 8 quarter-square triangles
- 2 squares, 9⅜" x 9⅜"; cut the squares in half diagonally to yield 4 half-square triangles

From the medium green fat quarter, cut:
- 8 bias strips, 1" x 15"
- Reserve the remainder of the fabric for the leaf appliqués.

From the blue binding fabric, cut:
- 7 strips, 2" x 42"

This is a great project for using all those fat quarters and fat eighths in your stash. There is only one block pattern, but the clever use of color makes each block look unique. Follow my exact color combinations if you want your lap quilt to look just like mine, or feel free to substitute your own favorite colors and have fun!

Cutting Template Pieces

1. Trace the A and B patterns onto template plastic or cardstock, making sure to trace the lines exactly. These patterns include a ¼" seam allowance. Write the piece letter on the template for later reference. Cut out the templates, cutting exactly on the drawn line.

2. To cut the A pieces, lay one blue 3⅝"-wide strip flat (not folded) on your cutting mat right side up. Using the A template, trace and then cut out 8 blue A pieces, being careful *not* to cut into the seam allowance when cutting the pieces apart. Cut 12 purple A pieces, 16 red A pieces, and 16 green A pieces.

3. Repeating step 2, cut 8 blue A reversed pieces, 12 purple A reversed pieces, 16 red A reversed pieces, and 16 green A reversed pieces.

4. Using the B template and the light tan 3⅝"-wide strips, trace and then cut out 28 light tan B pieces as shown. Use the medium tan 3⅝"-wide strips to cut out 24 medium tan B pieces. Be careful *not* to cut into the seam allowance when cutting the pieces apart.

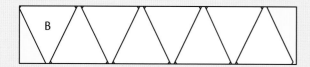

Making the Block Units

Each block is made up of six different units: star-point units, center pinwheel units, 1A units, 1B units, units 2, and units 3. The construction of each unit is described in this section. Use a ¼"-wide seam allowance throughout. After sewing each seam, press the seam allowances in the direction indicated by the arrows (or press them open).

STAR-POINT UNITS

1. With right sides together and raw edges aligned, join a green A piece to a light tan B piece.

2. With right sides together and raw edges aligned, join a green A reversed piece to the other side of the B piece as shown. The unit should measure 3½" x 3½". If you need to trim the unit, be sure to leave a ¼" seam allowance beyond the tan point. This will ensure that the points will not be cut off when assembling the block. Make eight green/light tan units.

Make 8.

3. Repeat steps 1 and 2 to make the following units:
   ✦ 8 units using green A pieces and medium tan B pieces
   ✦ 8 units using red A pieces and light tan B pieces
   ✦ 8 units using red A pieces and medium tan B pieces
   ✦ 12 units using purple A pieces and light tan B pieces
   ✦ 8 units using blue A pieces and medium tan B pieces

CENTER PINWHEEL UNITS

1. Refer to "Triangle Squares" on page 7. Draw a diagonal line from corner to corner on the wrong side of the light and medium tan C squares. Pair a C square with a brown D square, right sides together. Sew ¼" from both sides of the drawn line, and then cut the squares apart to make 52 triangle squares. The squares should measure 3½" x 3½".

Make 52.

2. Lay out four triangle squares as shown. Join the squares into rows, and then sew the rows together to make a pinwheel unit. The unit should measure 6½" x 6½". Make 13 units.

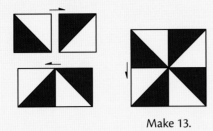

Make 13.

UNITS 1A AND 1B

Both units are constructed with a light or medium tan H rectangle, red or blue E rectangles, and red or blue F squares. Unit 1B is a mirror image of unit 1A.

1. To make unit 1A, join an E rectangle and an F square as shown. Then join the E/F unit to an H rectangle. Make the number of 1A units indicated of each color combination. Each unit should measure 3" x 3½".

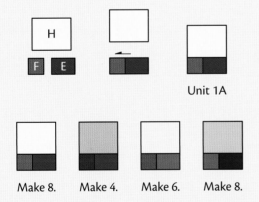

Make 8.   Make 4.   Make 6.   Make 8.

2. Repeat step 1 to make the number of 1B units indicated of each color combination.

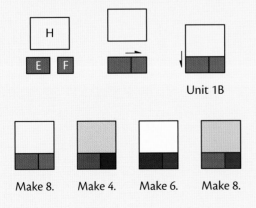

Make 8.   Make 4.   Make 6.   Make 8.

UNITS 2

Join a red or blue E rectangle to a light tan or medium tan G rectangle as shown. Make the number of units indicated for each color combination. Each unit should measure 2" x 3½".

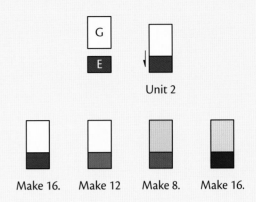

Make 16.   Make 12   Make 8.   Make 16.

UNITS 3

Join a light tan or medium tan I rectangle to a red or blue J square as shown. Make the number of units indicated for each color combination. Each unit should measure 2½" x 3½".

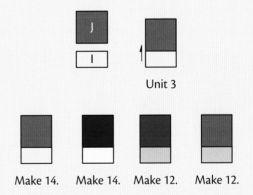

Make 14.   Make 14.   Make 12.   Make 12.

Making the Blocks

Before assembling the blocks, separate the units into stacks by color. For example, put all the light tan/green star-point units together and all the medium tan/green star-point units together. When laying out the units for a block, the star-points units should all match and the E rectangles should all be the same color. The blocks will have either a light tan or a medium tan background. The best way to make sure you have the right colors in a block is to lay out the pieces on a design wall. Upon completion, you'll have seven blocks with a light tan background and six blocks with a medium tan background. Refer to the photo for color-placement guidance.

1. Join a 1A unit and a 1B unit to a star-point unit as shown to make a row. Make 14 light tan rows and 12 medium tan rows.

   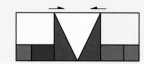

2. Join a blue/light tan unit 3 and a red/light tan unit 3 to a light tan row from step 1 as shown. Make 14 light tan rows. Repeat with the medium tan units and the medium tan rows from step 1. Make 12 medium tan rows.

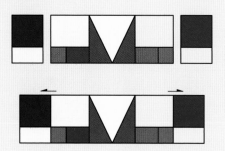

3. Join two of tan/red unit 2 to a star-point unit as shown. Make 16 light tan units and 8 medium tan units. Repeat to join tan/blue units to a star-point unit. Make 12 light tan units and 16 medium tan units.

 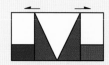

4. Join a unit from step 3 to either side of a center pinwheel unit as shown.

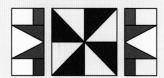 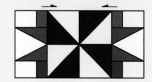

5. Lay out two rows from step 2 and one row from step 4 as shown. Sew the rows together to complete a block. The block should measure 12½" x 12½". Make a total of 13 blocks.

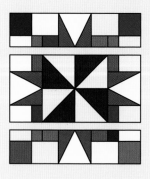 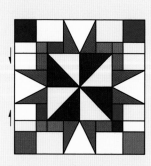

Make 13.

Assembling the Quilt Top

Before assembling the blocks, lay them out on the floor or a design wall. Rearrange the blocks until you're happy with the placement. The following instructions are for the layout shown in the photo on page 57.

1. Join dark brown quarter-square triangles to opposite sides of a light tan block to make a row. Make sure you align the 90° angle of the triangles with the bottom corners of the block. The tips of the triangles will extend beyond the top of the block. Do *not* trim the triangle tips. Join a dark brown half-square triangle to the top of the row. Make two rows.

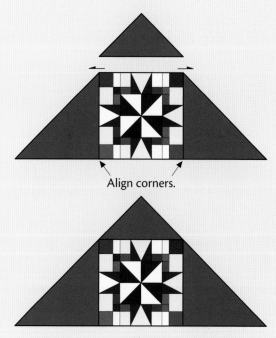

Align corners.

Make 2.

2. Join one light tan block and two medium tan blocks to make a row as shown. Join dark brown quarter-square triangles to the ends of the row as shown. Make two rows.

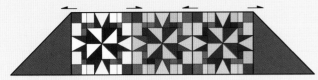

Make 2.

3. Join three light tan blocks and two medium tan blocks to make a row, alternating them as shown. Join dark brown half-square triangles to the ends of the row. Make one row.

Make 1.

4. Lay out the rows from steps 1, 2, and 3 as shown. Sew the rows together and press the seam allowances away from the center row. Trim and square up the quilt top, making sure to leave ¼" beyond the points of all the blocks for seam allowances.

5. Refer to "Border Strips" on page 11. Measure the length of your quilt top; it should be 51½". Trim four of the dark brown border strips to 26" long. Join the strips in pairs along the short ends to make two 51½"-long strips and sew them to the sides of the quilt top.

6. Measure the width of your quilt top (including the just-added borders); it should be 58". Trim the remaining dark brown strips to 29¼" long. Sew the strips together in pairs along the short ends to make two 58"-long strips and sew them to the top and bottom of the quilt top.

Adding the Appliqué

Use your preferred method of appliqué or refer to "Appliqué" on page 9 for more information on needle-turn appliqué and fusible-web machine appliqué. Refer to the diagram for appliqué placement.

1. Refer to "Making Bias Stems" on page 10 to make stems from the medium green bias strips. Appliqué the stems in place. The flower appliqués will cover the raw ends of the stems.

2. Using the patterns on page 63 and your preferred appliqué method, make the appliqué shapes from the fabrics indicated.

3. Appliqué the shapes in place, working in numerical order. (I've found it easier to appliqué the flower centers in place before appliquéing the flowers to the quilt top.)

Finishing the Quilt

Refer to "Finishing Techniques" on page 12 for instructions as needed.

1. Layer the quilt top with batting and backing; baste.

2. Quilt as desired. This quilt was professionally machine quilted by a long-arm quilter. She quilted an overall meandering pattern that included stars. She also echo quilted around the stems, leaves, and flowers to make them stand out.

3. Use the blue 2"-wide strips to bind the quilt.

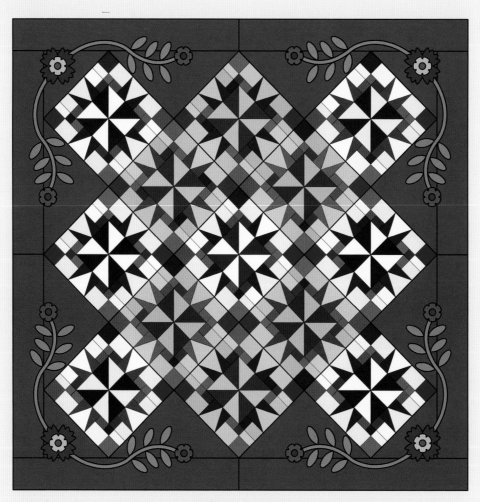

Appliqué placement

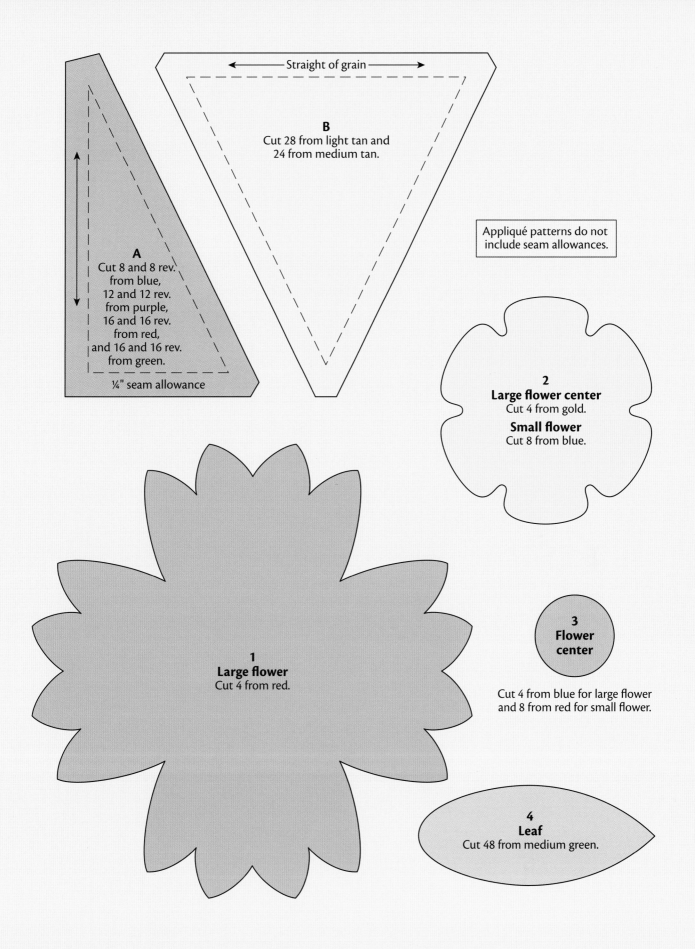

Straight of grain

B
Cut 28 from light tan and
24 from medium tan.

A
Cut 8 and 8 rev.
from blue,
12 and 12 rev.
from purple,
16 and 16 rev.
from red,
and 16 and 16 rev.
from green.

¼" seam allowance

Appliqué patterns do not
include seam allowances.

2
Large flower center
Cut 4 from gold.

Small flower
Cut 8 from blue.

1
Large flower
Cut 4 from red.

3
**Flower
center**

Cut 4 from blue for large flower
and 8 from red for small flower.

4
Leaf
Cut 48 from medium green.

Traveling Star

Finished Quilt Size: 74" x 74" • **Finished Block Size:** 12" x 12"

Quilted by Annette Ashbach of The Quiltmaker's Nest

Materials

Yardages are based on 42"-wide fabric. Fat quarters measure 18" x 21".

11 fat quarters of assorted tan fabrics for blocks

10 fat quarters of assorted green fabrics for blocks

7 fat quarters of assorted red fabrics for blocks

4 fat quarters of assorted blue fabrics for blocks

1 yard of tan fabric for inner border

½ yard of red fabric for middle border

⅞ yard of blue fabric for outer border

⅝ yard of red fabric for binding

4½ yards of backing fabric

82" x 82" piece of batting

Cutting

Cut strips across the width of the fabric. This quilt is made from two different blocks. The cutting instructions are listed separately for each block. To make assembling the blocks easier, be sure to label each piece with the piece and block number.

BLOCK 1

From the assorted tan fat quarters, cut a total of:
- 13 squares, 4½" x 4½" (A1)
- 104 squares, 2½" x 2½" (C1)
- 52 squares, 2⅞" x 2⅞" (G1)

From the assorted red fat quarters, cut a total of:
- 104 rectangles, 2½" x 4½" (B1)
- 104 squares, 2½" x 2½" (E1)

From the assorted green fat quarters, cut a total of:
- 52 squares, 2⅞" x 2⅞" (F1)
- 104 squares, 2½" x 2½" (D1)

BLOCK 2

From the assorted tan fat quarters, cut a total of:
- 6 squares, 5¼" x 5¼"; cut the squares into quarters diagonally to yield 24 quarter-square triangles (A2)
- 48 squares, 4½" x 4½" (E2)

From the assorted green fat quarters, cut a total of:
- 6 squares, 5¼" x 5¼"; cut the squares into quarters diagonally to yield 24 quarter-square triangles (B2)
- 192 squares, 2½" x 2½" (D2)

From the assorted blue fat quarters, cut a total of:
- 96 rectangles, 2½" x 4½" (C2)

From the tan border fabric, cut:
- 4 strips, 3½" x 33½"
- 4 strips, 3½" x 30½"

From the red border fabric, cut:
- 4 strips, 1½" x 34½"
- 4 strips, 1½" x 33½"

From the blue border fabric, cut:
- 4 strips, 3¼" x 37¼"
- 4 strips, 3¼" x 34½"

From the red binding fabric, cut:
- 8 strips, 2" x 42"

Making Block 1

After sewing each seam, press the seam allowances in the direction indicated by the arrows (or press them open).

1. Refer to "Folded-Corner Technique" on page 8. Draw a diagonal line from corner to corner on the wrong side of each tan C1 square. Use the marked squares and 52 of the red B1 rectangles to make 52 red/tan flying-geese units.

Make 52.

2. Repeat step 1 using the remaining red B1 rectangles and the green D1 squares to make 52 red/green flying-geese units.

Make 52.

I love creating a quilt design using two coordinating blocks to make a secondary design like I did with this lap quilt. I chose reds, greens, and blues for my colors; however, feel free to substitute your favorite three-color combination.

3. Refer to "Triangle Squares" on page 7. Draw a diagonal line from corner to corner on the wrong side of each tan G1 square. Pair a G1 square with a green F1 square, right sides together. Sew ¼" from both sides of the drawn line. Cut the squares apart to make two triangle squares, each measuring 2½" x 2½". Make a total of 104 triangle squares.

Make 104.

4. Join a triangle square from step 3 to each end of a red/green flying-geese unit from step 2 as shown. Make 26 of these rows.

Make 26.

5. Join a red E1 square to each end of a row from step 4 to complete row 1. Make 26 rows.

Row 1.
Make 26.

6. Join a red E1 square to each end of a red/tan flying-geese unit from step 1 as shown. Make 26 of these rows.

Make 26.

7. Join a triangle square from step 3 to each end of a row from step 6 to complete row 2. Make 26 rows.

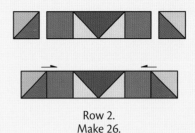

Row 2.
Make 26.

8. Join a red/tan flying-geese unit to opposite sides of a tan A1 square as shown. Then join a red/green flying-geese unit to each end of the row to complete row 3. Make 13 rows.

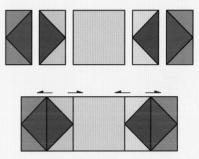

Row 3.
Make 13.

9. Lay out two of row 1, two of row 2, and one row 3 as shown. Sew the rows together to complete block 1. The block should measure 12½" x 12½". Make 13 blocks.

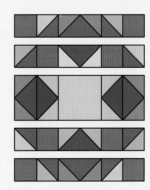

Block 1.
Make 13.

Making Block 2

1. Join a tan A2 triangle to a green B2 triangle as shown. Make 24 tan/green units.

Make 24.

2. Join two units from step 1 as shown to make a square unit. The unit should measure 4½" x 4½". Make 12 units.

Make 12.

3. Draw a diagonal line from corner to corner on the wrong side of each green D2 square. Use the marked squares and the blue C2 rectangles to make 96 blue/green flying-geese units as shown. Refer to "Folded-Corner Technique" as needed.

Make 96.

4. Join two flying-geese units from step 3 as shown. The unit should measure 4½" x 4½". Make 48 of these units.

Make 48.

5. Join tan E2 squares to opposite sides of the unit from step 4 to make row 1. Make 24 rows.

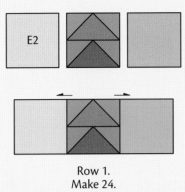

Row 1.
Make 24.

6. Join units from step 4 to opposite sides of a unit from step 2 to make row 2. Make 12 rows.

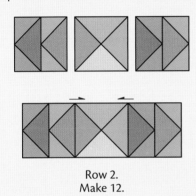

Row 2.
Make 12.

7. Lay out two of row 1 and one row 2 as shown. Sew the rows together to complete block 2. The block should measure 12½" x 12½". Make 12 blocks.

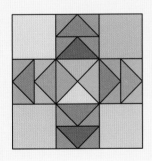

Block 2.
Make 12.

Assembling the Quilt Top

1. Lay out three of block 1 and two of block 2, alternating them as shown. Sew the blocks together to make row A. Press the seam allowances toward block 2 (or press them open). Make three rows.

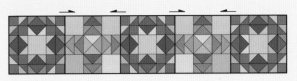

Row A.
Make 3.

2. Lay out three of block 2 and two of block 1, alternating them as shown. Sew the blocks together to make row B. Press the seam allowances toward block 2 (or press them open). Make two rows.

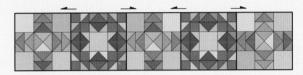

Row B.
Make 2.

3. Lay out the A and B rows, alternating them as shown. Sew the rows together and press the seam allowances in one direction (or press them open). The quilt top should measure 60½" x 60½".

Adding the Borders

Refer to "Border Strips" on page 11 as needed.

1. Join the tan 3½" x 30½" strips in pairs along the short ends to make two 60½"-long strips. Sew the strips to the sides of the quilt-top.

2. Join the tan 3½" x 33½" strips in pairs along the short ends to make two 66½"-long strips. Sew the strips to the top and bottom of the quilt top.

3. Repeat step 1 using the red 1½" x 33½" strips to make two 66½"-long strips. Repeat step 2 using the red 1½" x 34½" strips to make two 68½"-long strips. Sew the strips to the sides, and then to the top and bottom of the quilt top.

4. Repeat step 1 using the blue 3¼" x 34½" strips to make two 68½"-long strips. Repeat step 2 using the blue 3¼" x 37¼" strips to make two 74"-long strips. Sew the strips to the sides, and then to the top and bottom of the quilt top.

Finishing the Quilt

Refer to "Finishing Techniques" on page 12 for instructions as needed.

1. Layer the quilt top with batting and backing; baste.

2. Quilt as desired. This quilt was professionally machine quilted by a long-arm quilter. She quilted an overall meandering pattern that included stars.

3. Use the red 2"-wide strips to bind the quilt.

Star Maze

Finished Quilt Size: 62½" x 62½" • **Finished Block Size:** 12" x 12"

Quilted by Annette Ashbach of The Quiltmaker's Nest

Materials

Yardages are based on 42"-wide fabric. Fat quarters measure 18" x 21" and fat eighths measure 9" x 21".

8 fat quarters of assorted tan fabrics for blocks

2 yards of medium blue fabric for setting triangles and inner border

6 fat quarters of assorted dark fabrics for blocks

3 fat quarters of assorted medium fabrics for blocks

⅝ yard of dark blue fabric for outer border

⅜ yard of medium green fabric for leaf and flower calyx appliqués

1 fat quarter of dark green fabric for stem appliqués

1 fat quarter of medium purple fabric for large flower appliqués

2 fat eighths of assorted medium gold fabrics for large flower center and small flower appliqués

4" x 8" rectangle of dark red fabric for small flower-center appliqués

½ yard of medium or dark green fabric for binding

4¼ yards of backing fabric

71" x 71" piece of batting

Cutting

Cut strips across the width of the fabric unless instructed otherwise. Refer to "Cutting Triangles" on page 28 for instructions on cutting triangles. Refer to "Making Bias Stems" on page 10 for instructions on cutting bias strips.

From the assorted medium fat quarters, cut a total of:
+ 104 squares, 2½" x 2½" (B)

From the assorted dark fat quarters, cut a total of:
+ 13 squares, 4½" x 4½" (A)
+ 52 rectangles, 2½" x 4½" (C)
+ 104 squares, 2½" x 2½" (F)

From the assorted tan fat quarters, cut a total of:
+ 52 rectangles, 2½" x 8½" (E)
+ 156 squares, 2½" x 2½" (D)

From the medium blue fabric, cut:
+ 8 strips, 4½" x 42"
+ 2 squares, 18¼" x 18¼"; cut the squares into quarters diagonally to yield 8 quarter-square triangles
+ 2 squares, 9⅜" x 9⅜"; cut the squares in half diagonally to yield 4 half-square triangles

From the dark blue fabric, cut:
+ 8 strips, 2" x 42"

From the dark green fat quarter, cut:
+ 8 bias strips, 1" x 12½"

From the medium or dark green binding fabric, cut:
+ 7 strips, 2" x 42"

Making the Blocks

Refer to "Folded-Corner Technique" on page 8. After sewing each seam, press the seam allowances in the direction indicated by the arrows (or press them open).

1. Draw a diagonal line from corner to corner on the wrong side of 52 of the medium B squares. Lay a marked square on the upper-right corner of a dark A square, right sides together. Sew along the line and trim the excess fabric, leaving a ¼" seam allowance.

2. Repeat step 1, adding marked B squares to the remaining three corners of the A square to make a center unit. The unit should measure 4½" square. Make 13.

Make 13.

This is a great lap quilt for using up all of those colorful fat quarters or for giving yourself an excuse to buy more! If you want an even scrappier look, substitute two fat eighths for one fat quarter. This simple quilt design is one repeating block, set on point, to create an interesting secondary design. The added floral appliqué completes the quilt.

3. Draw a diagonal line from corner to corner on the wrong side of 104 of the tan D squares. Use the marked D squares and the dark C rectangles to make 52 flying-geese units as shown.

Make 52.

4. Join a medium B square to each end of a flying-geese unit from step 3 to make a row. Make 26 of these rows.

Make 26.

5. Join flying-geese units from step 3 to opposite sides of a center unit from step 2 to make a row as shown. Make 13 of these rows.

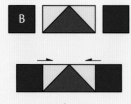

Make 13.

6. Lay out two rows from step 4 and one row from step 5 as shown. Sew the rows together to make a larger center unit. The unit should measure 8½" square. Make 13 of these units.

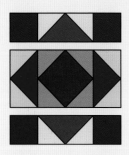

Make 13.

7. Draw a diagonal line from corner to corner on the wrong side of the dark F squares. Lay a marked square on one end of a tan E rectangle, right sides together, as shown. Sew along the line and trim the excess fabric, leaving a ¼" seam allowance. Sew a marked F square on the other end of the E rectangle as shown to complete the unit. Make 52 of these units.

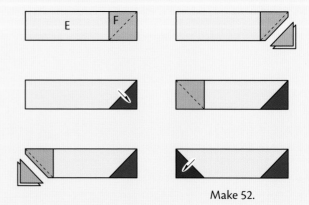

Make 52.

8. Join a tan D square to each end of an E/F unit from step 7 to make a row. Make 26 of these rows.

Make 26.

9. Join E/F units from step 7 to opposite sides of a unit from step 6 to make a row. Make 13 of these rows.

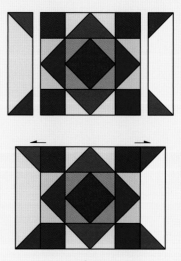

Make 13.

10. Lay out two rows from step 8 and one row from step 9 as shown. Sew the rows together to complete the block. The blocks should measure 12½" square. Make 13 blocks.

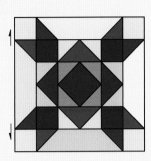

Make 13.

Assembling the Quilt Top

1. Join medium blue quarter-square triangles to opposite sides of a block as shown to make a row. Make sure you align the 90° angle of the triangles with the bottom corners of the block. The tips of the triangles will extend beyond the top of the block. Do *not* trim the triangle tips. Join a medium blue half-square triangle to the top of the row. Make two rows.

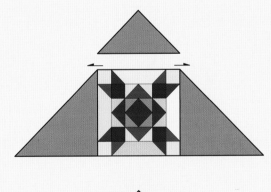

Make 2.

2. Join three blocks to make a row. Join medium blue quarter-square triangles to the ends of the row as shown. Make two rows.

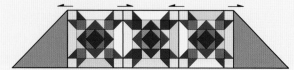

Make 2.

3. Join five blocks to make a row. Join medium blue half-square triangles to the ends of the row as shown. Make one row.

Make 1.

4. Lay out the rows from steps 1, 2, and 3 as shown. Sew the rows together and press the seam allowances away from the center row. Trim and square up the quilt top, making sure to leave ¼" beyond the points of all the blocks for seam allowances.

5. Refer to "Border Strips" on page 11. For the inner border, measure the length of your quilt top; it should be 51½". Trim four of the medium blue strips to 26" long. Join the strips in pairs along the short ends to make two 51½"-long strips and sew them to the sides of the quilt top.

6. Measure the width of your quilt top (including the just-added borders); it should be 59½". Trim the remaining medium blue strips to 30" long. Sew the strips together in pairs along the short ends to make two 59½"-long strips and sew them to the top and bottom of the quilt top.

7. For the outer border, measure the length of your quilt top; it should be 59½". Trim four of the dark blue strips to 30" long. Join the strips in pairs along the short ends to make two 59½"-long strips and sew them to the sides of the quilt top.

8. Measure the width of your quilt top (including the just-added borders); it should be 62½". Trim the remaining dark blue strips to 31½" long. Sew the strips together in pairs along the short ends to make two 62½"-long strips and sew them to the top and bottom of the quilt top.

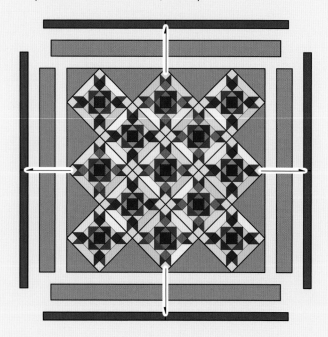

Adding the Appliqué

Use your preferred method of appliqué or refer to "Appliqué" on page 9 for more information on needle-turn hand appliqué and fusible-web machine appliqué. Refer to the diagram for appliqué placement.

1. Refer to "Making Bias Stems" on page 10 to make stems from the dark green bias strips. Appliqué them in place. The flower appliqués will cover the raw ends of the stems.

2. Using the patterns on page 78 and your preferred method of appliqué, make the appliqué shapes from the fabrics indicated.

3. Appliqué the shapes in place, working in numerical order. (I've found it easier to appliqué the flower centers in place before appliquéing the flowers to the quilt top.)

Finishing the Quilt

Refer to "Finishing Techniques" on page 12 for instructions as needed.

1. Layer the quilt top with batting and backing; baste.

2. Quilt as desired. This quilt was professionally machine quilted by a long-arm quilter. She quilted an overall meandering pattern that included stars. She echo quilted around the stems, leaves, and flowers to make them stand out.

3. Use the medium or dark green 2"-wide strips to bind the quilt.

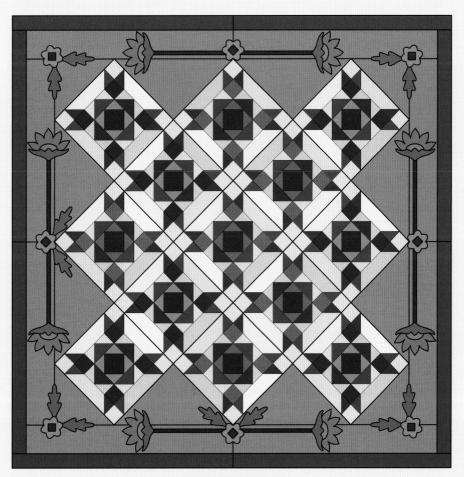

Appliqué placement

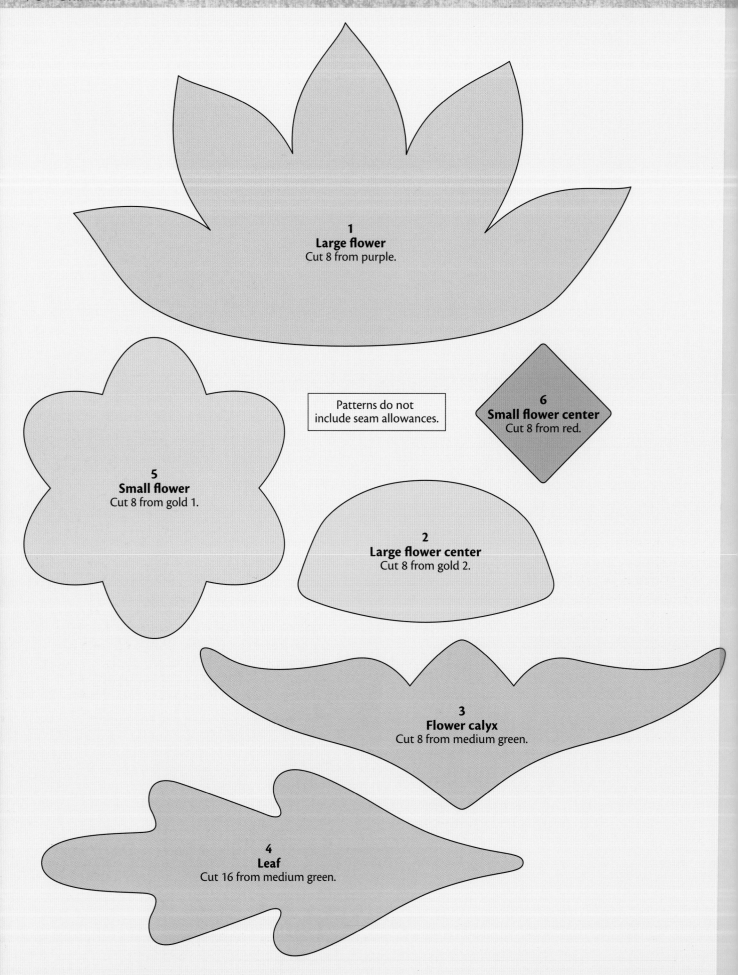

1
Large flower
Cut 8 from purple.

Patterns do not
include seam allowances.

6
Small flower center
Cut 8 from red.

5
Small flower
Cut 8 from gold 1.

2
Large flower center
Cut 8 from gold 2.

3
Flower calyx
Cut 8 from medium green.

4
Leaf
Cut 16 from medium green.

About the Author

Deanne Eisenman caught the quilting bug by taking a beginner's class more than 20 years ago for something to do. Since then, there has been no looking back. Any other hobby paled in comparison. When she could not find a pattern she wanted in a quilt shop, out came the graph paper and pencil, and a new design was born. Deanne began her pattern company, Snuggles Quilts, in 2003 and has been successfully self-publishing her patterns for several years. A number of her patterns have been published in major quilting magazines and quilt calendars. This is her second book with Martingale & Company.

Deanne lives and works from her home in Osage, Iowa. Her family includes her husband, Craig; her daughter, Ali, a college sophomore; and her son, Mitch, a junior in high school. Also at home is the company namesake, Snuggles the cat, who thinks she owns the sewing room and the company. She usually can be found curled up on top of the fabric or batting stash in the closet. At this point, her only contribution seems to be the cat hair she leaves behind! Starting the pattern company and writing quilt-pattern books has been a dream come true for Deanne. She says it's great to go to work every day and love what you're doing!

THERE'S MORE ONLINE!

Browse Deanne's extensive pattern line at www.snugglequilts.com. Find more great quilt books and patterns at www.martingale-pub.com.

You might also enjoy these other fine titles from
Martingale & Company

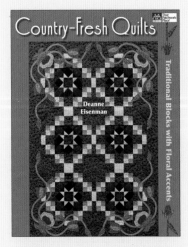

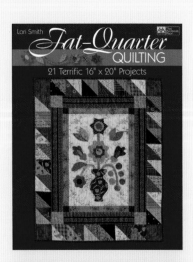

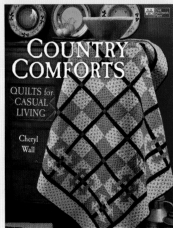

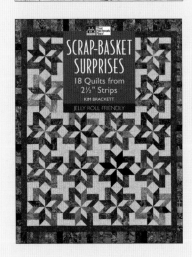

Our books are available at bookstores and your favorite craft, fabric, and yarn retailers.
Visit us at www.martingale-pub.com or contact us at:

1-800-426-3126
International: 1-425-483-3313
Fax: 1-425-486-7596
Email: info@martingale-pub.com

America's Best-Loved Quilt Books®

America's Best-Loved Craft & Hobby Books®
America's Best-Loved Knitting Books®